Bankruptcy 101

An Insider's Guide to Filing
Chapter 7 Bankruptcy
by Yourself Without
an Attorney

Michael Greiner, J.D.

LIMIT OF LIABILITY/DISCLAIMER OF WARRANTY

Bankruptcy 101

An Insider's Guide to Filing
Chapter 7 Bankruptcy
by Yourself Without
an Attorney

Michael Greiner, J.D.

Printed in the United States of America

ISBN: 978-1-935254-30-0

Cover Design by Vorris Dee Justesen
Book Design by Nadene Carter

First printing, 2010

Dedication

For Madilyn, the love of my life, the reason I do what I do.

Table of Contents

Introduction

*T*he word Bankruptcy brings up strong feelings. Many people don't realize Bankruptcy is actually in the U.S. Constitution, and that Walt Disney, Donald Trump (through companies owned by him), Ulysses S. Grant, Willie Nelson, Mark Twain, Larry King, and even Abraham Lincoln all filed Bankruptcy. In other words, if you need to file Bankruptcy, you're in good company. The people listed above ended up with major success post-Bankruptcy.

That's the reality of Bankruptcy. When you get in over your head, Bankruptcy gives you a chance to make a fresh start and keeps your creditors from tearing your life apart. Many people say our Bankruptcy laws are a major factor behind the American economy's long-term strength. In much of Europe and Japan, recessions lingered for years and economic growth has been stymied because people and companies couldn't get out from under their debts. That's not to say Bankruptcy should be our first choice, but it should be a choice.

In truth, Bankruptcy is a tool. If you're in a situation where creditors make you miserable with garnishments, lawsuits, and other collections, it benefits all of us if you get out from under that debt and back into activity with the U.S. economy. That's why Bankruptcy laws exist.

During the past few years I've represented over a thousand people in Bankruptcy, so I feel I have a good sense of the environment. In this book, I tell you the realities as I see them. You'll soon notice what you read here is the exact opposite of what the banks want you to believe. For example, banks never tell you how quickly your credit score will bounce back.

As a Bankruptcy attorney, I know this is a complex and difficult process. Nevertheless, some people want to file Bankruptcy without an attorney's assistance. That is your right, and I'm offering you the information and tools to go through this on your own. If you're one of those people, then this book is for you.

Even if you want an attorney to assist you in filing Chapter 7 Bankruptcy, this book will help you understand the process. If you want a comprehensive and understandable primer on Bankruptcy, then this book is for you.

If nothing else, I hope this book helps people stand up to the banks. Don't feel bad about looking out for your own interests, because the banks won't be looking out for you. We should no longer feel banks hold all the power, nor should we allow them to walk all over us. The threat of Bankruptcy should be enough to get the attention of a creditor, because Bankruptcy is the one place where you have rights too.

Know your rights and use them. That's what this book is about.

Chapter 1

Don't Feel Bad for the Banks

When I first realized credit card companies and banks don't care about me, it came as quite a shock. Of course, I knew intellectually these for-profit, public corporations must put their shareholders' interests first. But I believed they were honorable corporate citizens, fair dealers in an economy where the myth of capitalism thrives, where loyalty and a handshake still mean something, and where the long-term good is a consideration. I was wrong.

I guess you could say I was a little slow on the uptake since it took two incidents before I came to understand how unscrupulous the large banks are. Like most people, I was so steeped in the culture of laissez-faire that I couldn't believe banks would operate in this way.

The first incident came as I prepared to establish my law practice. At the time, I'd been working in a cushy government job for a decade. The paycheck was steady and the benefits good, but I was never going to get rich as a bureaucrat. So I decided to chase the American dream. Having read the statistics, I knew the primary reason most new businesses fail was due to lack of start-up capital. To address this problem, I formed a plan.

Over the years, I'd developed an outstanding credit rating. The credit limits on one card in particular kept going up as I faithfully made payments on time. But so did the balance. By the time I wanted to start my business, my limit and my balance on this card exceeded $30,000. So it seemed logical that if I paid off this card, I'd have another $30,000 in credit to use over the next year as start-up capital. With that in mind, I emptied the deferred compensation account I'd been accumulating over the past ten years and handed the funds over to the bank, thinking myself very clever.

You can imagine my surprise when, upon cashing my check, the bank immediately closed the account and wouldn't even let me charge a hamburger with that card. I called the customer service line and reminded them of my loyalty, told them about my many years of faithfully paying my bill, and explained I'd just liquidated my savings to pay them. None of it mattered. They didn't care.

Fortunately, due to my good credit rating, I had other credit cards and was able to cobble together enough credit to start my practice. I thought the behavior of this other creditor was simply an aberration. Boy, was I wrong.

As my practice grew, I started to rely more and more on one credit card in particular. Much of what I charged were court filing fees. Many courts have been moving to electronic filing over the Internet. To use this service, attorneys need to have a credit card on which they can charge the filing fees. Clients would typically pay these fees up-front, so the funds were there to pay the debt. Every month, as I filed more and more cases, the debt on this one card went up. But since I had already received the filing fees from my clients, I was able to pay it off every month. Month after month, I charged more and more on this credit card, and then paid it off, on time, every month. This seemed like a great arrangement, because this particular card gave me great benefits. When I took my family on a vacation to Hawaii one year, much of that vacation was paid for by points from this bank. As a result, I started paying more and more bills with the credit card. I paid my phone bill, advertising expenses, and Internet service. I knew the account number and expiration date by heart from entering them into web sites so often. Every month, I accumulated tens of thousands of dollars of debt on that card, and every month, I paid it off.

Then one month, out of the blue, that creditor suddenly cut me off. I called them, uttering the plea I would hear again and again in my practice: "I've been a loyal customer. I've always done what you asked of me, and now you're abandoning me." I was hurt at first, then angry, and finally I learned my lesson.

Ironically, when both these incidents occurred I was an attorney who'd worked in responsible government and private sector management positions for nearly twenty years. Indeed, I'd always been interested in bankruptcy law, and when I started my practice that's the field in which I specialized. But I still fell prey to the beliefs I hear expressed in my office by prospective clients every day: "We do what the banks ask of us and behave honorably toward them. Shouldn't they behave the same way toward us?" Unfortunately, the answer is: "No."

Every day in my office I hear similar stories. People tell me about losing a job, having a business fail, going through a divorce, succumbing to an addiction, enduring a serious illness, or some other tragedy. They always made their payments on time. They paid off their creditors, again and again. They had high credit ratings. They wanted to pay back their debts. So they did what they thought was the responsible thing: they called their creditors and explained the situation. They made reasonable requests, asking for a little more time, a little less interest, a slightly lower payment, just to get them through this difficult time. But the banks almost always said no. They wanted their money now. They said, "Make a payment, then we'll consider a change." The people made the payment, and the bank still said no. My clients begged and pleaded. They explained that if the bank wouldn't work with them, they'd have no choice but to file for bankruptcy, and then the bank would get nothing. They pointed to their history and long loyalty to the bank as a demonstration of good faith. But the banks still said no. Usually, to their shock and dismay, the people ended up in a bankruptcy attorney's office because they felt they had no other choice.

Most of the time it's true: They don't have any other choice. Sadly, many of these people have drained 401Ks and IRAs to stay current on credit card debt. The funds meant for their retirement savings went to pay interest. And they still ended up in the same situation they were in when they started. Many people made credit card payments rather than house or car payments, ending up still in debt, also facing foreclosure on their home or repossession of their vehicle. All my clients played by the rules, as I did, only to find these rules don't apply to the banks.

All of us grew up steeped in a culture that celebrates private enterprise. We watch bank commercials that emphasize how much they care about us. We watched *It's a Wonderful Life* where Jimmy Stewart worked with his bank's customers, allowing them to make payment arrangements on their debts when they ran into hard times. We believe we should be responsible and honorable, and if we are, others will behave the same way. But that isn't the case with the banks.

Take the recent recession. This recession was basically created by the banks through greed and irresponsible risk-taking. The banks leant mortgages to people who were unable to pay them over the long term. They got people to sign on the dotted line by writing adjustable rate mortgages. The initial rate was low enough so the borrower could afford, often barely afford, to make the payments. Within three years, the rate jumped to a more reasonable sum. The borrowers were told not to worry – they could refinance the mortgage before the rate increased. Believing the expert mortgage broker, the borrower signed and took the money with that intention. After all, the borrowers reasoned, why would they give us money if they didn't think we'd be able to repay it? Jimmy Stewart wouldn't have done that.

What we didn't realize, however, is the banks weren't actually lending their own money. They had no skin in the game. At every step was a salesman trying to make his commission. The mortgage broker was just a salesman, making a hefty commission for lending as much money as possible to as many people as possible. Once the borrower signed on the dotted line, the mortgage broker moved out of the picture. What about the bank to whom we make our payments, you ask? They lose out if we don't make our payments, don't they? No. In fact most people are making their mortgage payments to a servicer, someone who accepts your payments, takes a commission, and sends on the rest of the payment to the actual owner of the mortgage. So who owns the mortgage? Not the broker, and probably not even his or her employer. The broker would immediately sell the mortgage to one bank, then another, then another. At each step, the mortgage was packaged up, along with more and more similar mortgages, and split up as investments: bonds. That's what the banks call "securitizing" the mortgages. At each step, of course, commissions get paid. Eventually, various investors buy these bonds that represent a certain share of a large pot of mortgages. These are the people who eventually end up with your mortgage payments.

Who are these investors? They're often banks, life insurance companies, or pension funds. When you buy life insurance, for example, the insurance company has to invest your premiums to make sure it has the funds to pay out when you die. Similarly, pension funds need to invest each year to make sure funds are available for the payments when you retire. These are just two examples of many. The point is, these investors are far removed from your original mortgage broker and even more from the bank you send your payments to every month. These relationships are governed by complex legal contracts developed with an eye for protecting the property of the investors, but not with an eye for working with the original borrowers whose mortgages are tiny pieces of a huge pie split up between major institutional investors.

Residential mortgage backed securities, the bonds or investments that represent a share of this huge pie, used to be secure investments for these institutions. Typically, only a small percentage of people defaulted on their home mortgages. After all, home ownership is a big part of the American dream, and people would do just about anything to keep their homes. What's more, we've always been told to view our homes as an investment, a safe place to put our money rather than wasting it on rent. So as certain mortgage brokers, like the now defunct Countrywide, started writing more and more loans for more families, investors waited in the wings to snap up the bonds. They didn't worry about whether or not homeowners could make their payments over the long term. Fannie Mae and Freddie Mac, government-backed private companies that invest in mortgages, did ask those questions – but then they had trouble finding mortgages to buy, because so many other investors were willing to look the other way. To stay in the game, they lowered their standards… substantially. With so much money to be made in mortgage securities, everyone jumped on the train. Insurance companies like AIG started selling insurance to the investors in case their investments went bad, never expecting to have to pay on it. Investment banks like Lehman Brothers invested their profits from packaging up these mortgages and selling shares of them in the profitable bonds. They didn't want to miss out on the party. Mortgage brokers were making money from commissions, the servicers made money from commissions, and the investment banks who bundled the mortgages and sold shares of the big pie to investors were making money from commissions. Everyone was happy, right?

What started the collapse was probably imperceptible at first. Someone defaulted on a mortgage. The house went into foreclosure. At first this was no big deal, because, as always, the home was sold at a Sheriff's sale and the mortgage paid off. But a home sold by the mortgage company usually fetches a lower value than if sold by the homeowner. After all, the homeowner is a home's best sales-person. The homeowner keeps the house in tip-top shape to show it off to potential buyers. The homeowner talks up the house in the neighborhood, and is willing to wait until a good offer comes along. None of that happens when a mortgage company sells the property.

To the mortgage company, a house is an expense, not a home. They must pay to keep the place heated and cooled, keep the electricity and water on, and maintain the property. The sooner they can sell the house, the sooner the mortgage company cuts its losses. Furthermore, the dispossessed homeowner feels no need to keep the house up for the mortgage company. In many cases, angry homeowners strip the home of anything they can use in their new house. As a result, by the time someone buys the home, it often needs a lot of work.

Neighborhoods help determine housing values. If you own a home worth $200,000 and a similar home next to you sells for $100,000, now your home is worth something closer to $100,000. When a foreclosure happened and the house sold at a fraction of its earlier value, suddenly all the houses in the neighborhood were worth slightly less than before. If people in that neighborhood wanted to refinance their homes to avoid the big jump in payment with the adjustable rate mortgage, they no longer had enough equity in their home to refinance. Continuing with the earlier analogy, if a home was worth $200,000 and the homeowner refinanced three years earlier for $180,000 – that would have been a conservative mortgage back then, but it illustrates our scenario. Now, if the home next door sold for $100,000, then the $200,000 home is only valued at $150,000. Therefore, the home's value is less than what it would take to refinance it. The bank can't write a mortgage, because if the owner defaulted there wouldn't be enough equity to repay the investors. Through no fault of your own, you could be stuck with an adjustable rate mortgage you can't refinance, and the payment is about to jump to a level you can't afford. Soon, you're foreclosed upon, too.

Each foreclosure multiplies the problem. Every time a house gets foreclosed upon and gets sold for below-market value, that sale decreases the value of the other homes in the neighborhood. Suddenly, other people can no longer refinance their adjustable rate mortgages because they don't have enough equity there to protect the investors in case of default. More and more people can't refinance their adjustable rate mortgages as they intended to, leading to more and more foreclosures. You can see how it becomes an endless loop that feeds on itself.

In the days of *It's a Wonderful Life,* at some point, cooler heads would have prevailed. After all, it makes more sense for the bank to give the homeowner a break and get its payments rather than foreclosing and getting a fraction of what is owed, doesn't it? The problem is, who would step in? Not the mortgage broker who originally sold you the mortgage and promised you'd be able to refinance in three years. Not the servicer to whom you send a payment every month – they just accept your money and pass it on. Not the investment bank that packaged your mortgage with all those other mortgages and sold shares of that big pie to investors. Not even the final investors can do anything and who really get hurt, because they don't know what portion of which pie your mortgage is part of.

This quickly becomes an out-of-control train hurtling off the bridge. Our economy is so inter-connected that the financial crisis soon extended to every corner of our country. When people default on their mortgages, they can no longer finance cars or other major purchases. Then the manufacturers are in trouble. Mortgage brokers can no longer write mortgages since no one qualifies, so they lose their jobs. Realtors can no longer sell homes, because property values have declined due to the increasing number of foreclosures. Homes won't sell for enough to pay off the mortgages. Investors who counted on mortgage-backed securities as safe investments stop investing in mortgages, so people can no longer purchase homes. Builders go out of business, because people are no longer purchasing homes. Everyone is affected. People who used to work in dozens of industries no longer have money to spend on vacations, new cars, appliances, or other non-essential products and services. Even government gets into trouble, because with less income people pay less taxes. Government workers are laid off. Before you know it, a couple of foreclosures turn into the great recession of the late 2000s, and we have no idea how or when it will end.

The federal government and the Federal Reserve Board stepped in to try and avert this crisis. In some ways they succeeded, but in other ways, not so much. On the one hand, most economists agree things would have been worse without the rescue efforts of the federal government.

On the other hand, the steps taken by government – and the steps not taken – clearly illuminated the reality about banks in this country. The truth is, banks don't have to play by the rules, because if they don't like the rules they just ask Congress to change them.

When the crisis first spiraled out of control, banks ran to the government asking to be saved. At first, the Federal Reserve jumped to the rescue, as with AIG, the insurance company that had insured all these real estate investments without assets to back up the guarantees. But then, because of public outrage over this blatant effort to protect bad behavior, the Fed refused to save Lehman Brothers, who made unbelievable profits packaging, selling, and investing in mortgages. But then, realizing the government wouldn't save everyone, the stock market cratered. The government's response was to forget about the Lehman Brothers approach and save everyone big enough to impact the stock market. The problem is, the government now saves all the big banks, while allowing millions of people to lose their homes.

So we bailed out the banks. Most of them are now making profits as a result of the bailout, and they're hoping to pay back the small portion of the aid they received in the form of loans so they can go back to giving their executives excessive bonuses and trips to the Bahamas. One would think the extraordinary assistance we gave to the banks would be repaid with some sense of gratitude, some sense on the part of banks that they, who originally caused this crisis and were rescued by the American taxpayers, should play some part in fixing it. If you thought that, you'd be wrong.

In a recent speech, the President expressed the frustration of the American people with banks. He told the banks that since they benefited from the generosity of Congress, they should start lending again to small businesses, homeowners, and others on Main Street to help get the economy going. The banks basically ignored that plea and have put many small businesses in receivership by cutting off their lines of credit. But that isn't the worst part.

There is a solution to this crisis, and many bankruptcy attorneys such as myself have been talking about it for years. The fundamental problem in the economy right now, as I described above, is there's no way to realistically adjust mortgages to a decent interest rate and a reasonable value. Someone has to play the role of Jimmy Stewart and come up with a reasonable resolution, one in which the bank gets most of its money back and the homeowner gets to keep his home. There's a place where such deals have been done for years: Bankruptcy Court. A provision in the Bankruptcy Code allows judges to "cram down" debts like mortgages and car loans. The banks, of course, hate this provision. In the 1990s and early 2000s, they lobbied Congress to limit the cases where car loans could be crammed down. And even before that, a provision in the Code allowed cram downs on real estate mortgages, except where the real estate is your primary home. As a result, if you're a business and you file bankruptcy, we can reduce your interest rate, reduce your payment, and reduce the balance on the mortgage based upon the current value of the property. But for homeowners, we can't do that.

The proposal was to simply get rid of that limitation. Bankruptcy judges and attorneys are used to dealing with property valuations and cram downs, since those elements have been part of the process for years. Finally, a third party could step in and come up with a reasonable resolution. The process was in place: all they needed to do was change one sentence in the Bankruptcy Code.

Shortly after the election of 2008, when the Democrats took control of Congress and the White House, it seemed this proposal was destined to pass. First it passed the House of Representatives with a huge majority. Vice-President Joe Biden expressed his support for this plan during one of the debates, and the White House pledged to support it. But then the banks, after we spent hundreds of billions of dollars saving them, spent over a hundred million dollars lobbying Congress against this policy change. And the Senate, despite the Democratic super-majority, defeated the plan by one vote.

Emboldened by their success, the banks have fought off every effort to limit their greed. They apparently want their cake and want to eat it too. They lobby against everything that would protect us from another crisis. They lobby against everything that would limit their ability to charge outrageous interest rates. They even lobby against every bill that would limit the pay of their executives to something reasonable.

At first, I was amazed Congress would listen to the banks after all the problems they caused and all the help they received. But then I realized the banks truly are running this country. They, along with their partners in crime – the insurance companies – have purchased the best Congress money can buy. The Republicans, their preferred party, are blatant in their belief that banks and insurance companies should be allowed to steal as much as they want and get away with it. However, Democrats are also part of the problem. After all, the Democrats were the ones in charge when many of the so-called reforms passed that allowed this crisis to happen. Democrats could have passed the cram down legislation. And Democrats could easily have voted to stop the excesses of the banking industry and its executives. But they didn't.

The reason for this failure goes back to Watergate. After the Watergate crisis came to light, in the 1974 and 1976 elections, Democrats won huge margins in the House of Representatives in Congress. The leadership was aware of the fact that many of these new members of Congress represented Republican districts. So to protect them, the Congressional leadership embarked on a policy of selling "access" to Democratic members of Congress to the big financial power players, the banks and insurance companies. Yes, they told these traditionally Republican groups: "You may not like us as much as you like Republicans, but we're in charge. If you want to be able to talk with us and impact legislation, you'd better contribute heavily to our campaigns."

That's what the Democratic Congressional leadership told the banks and insurance companies. And realizing the harm Congress could do to them, the banks and insurance companies played along, giving so much money to the Democratic members of Congress that the Democrats were able to maintain their majority in the House of Representatives for twenty years.

Over time, a cozy relationship developed between the groups: one that exists to this day. When Ronald Reagan came along and articulated a political rationale for the "steal everything you can" goal of the Republicans, the Democrats were happy to go along, with a few tweaks here and there. It should come as no surprise that the first Democratic President after Reagan appointed Robert Rubin as his Secretary of the Treasury. Rubin was a former investment banker who opposed regulating the kind of investments that caused the current financial meltdown. He was also one of the biggest Democratic fundraisers in the country. Did Robert Rubin do a good job? Perhaps. But he represented the connection between the banking industry and the Democratic party. In this environment, who could be counted on to represent the interests of the American people when they diverge from the interests of the banking and insurance industries? The answer is: nobody.

Only one place is left where people can stand up to the banks with some protection, and that is Bankruptcy Court. You should know that banks and other creditors do have certain rights in the Bankruptcy Court, and those rights have to be protected and respected. But unlike everywhere else in today's America, average people also have rights there.

Not surprisingly, banks hate the Bankruptcy Court. Also not surprisingly, banks have lobbied year after year to limit the powers of those courts, as I described above. In October 2005, a major reform of the Bankruptcy Code was passed, giving banks many things they'd been lobbying for. Ironically, that reform bill was called the *Bankruptcy Abuse Prevention and Consumer Protection Act* – a lie if ever there was one. Be that as it may, despite all the misinformation published by the media about this legislation, most people can still file Chapter 7 Bankruptcy; most people can keep all their property through a Chapter 7 Bankruptcy; and the Bankruptcy Code still contains significant protections for average people.

Every day when I meet with prospective clients, I hear again and again how terrible people feel about filing bankruptcy against their banks. I don't think anyone should feel bad for the banks. Believe me, banks will take care of themselves. We need to establish a new kind of relationship with the banks: one that recognizes the important place they play in our economy as providers of credit, but one that doesn't expect them to play fair. You must protect yourself in dealing with the banks, and you have few tools available to do so.

Proof of the banks' loathing toward Bankruptcy is evidenced by the shocking lengths they go to in an effort to keep you from filing Bankruptcy. In my opinion, the biggest outrage of late was the public relations effort aimed at convincing people that, even without this legislation, banks will work with people to help them keep their homes. I believe this effort is public relations to stop Congress from stepping in and passing substantive legislation once and for all. I've represented too many people who've been led on by a bank, told the bank would modify their mortgage to reduce their payments and help them keep their homes, only to have the bank drag its feet and eventually foreclose. Even where the bank does agree to a modification, that modification is usually so minimal it does nothing to help the homeowners keep their property over the long-term. In my opinion, the number of times the banks actually modify the mortgages in a helpful way is tiny, but their PR flacks trumpet those modifications to such an extent that people believe banks might actually be working to help people. From what I've seen, mortgage modification programs are nothing more than window dressing.

The debt consolidation or debt settlement programs you see advertised on television are another example of this effort. They claim you can avoid the harm of Bankruptcy by working with them. What they don't tell you is, these companies don't work. Here's why: When you sign on, the company sets up a bank account for you. Every month you make a payment to that bank account rather than paying your credit cards. Of course, the first funds into the bank account go to pay your fees to the company, which are typically high. While you're making these payments instead of paying your credit cards, the banks don't sit idly by. They call you incessantly, harass you, send threatening letters, and eventually sue you. These companies don't tell you that debt consolidation offers you no protection from collection efforts. The theory is that eventually the bank will give up on its collection efforts and settle the debt for less than you owe. If you've accumulated sufficient funds in your account to do so, the consolidation company will cut a check to the bank, closing that account. In theory, by making these payments monthly you can settle all your debts – if you can put up with the harassment.

Here's the reality of this approach: many clients come into my office who are making payments to one of these companies and are now having their wages garnished by creditors. These companies don't tell you that can happen. If they're successful in getting one or more creditors to settle your debt, then the difference between what you owe and what the bank is willing to settle for is considered taxable income and you'll have to pay taxes on that amount. Furthermore, this process is entirely voluntary, so some banks simply won't settle. Finally, this process hurts your credit score worse than Bankruptcy. Let me explain.

It's true that Bankruptcy will hurt your credit. According to recent reports, the typical Chapter 7 will cut your credit score by 150 to 200 points. However, based on what I've seen, that reduction depends upon your credit score at filing. In my experience, a Bankruptcy won't reduce your credit score much below the mid-500s. Missing a payment to a creditor only impacts your credit score by 20-30 points. But that's only half the story. Each time you miss a payment to a creditor, you get that 20-30 point hit. As a result, if you have four credit cards and stop paying on them all, each month you experience an 80 to 120 point cut. Within two months you've exceeded the damage that would be done to your credit score with a Bankruptcy.

My clients are surprised at how quickly their credit scores bounce back. Most of my clients who follow a few simple steps are in the mid- to high-600s or even higher within a year of filling Bankruptcy. A good credit score is anything over 680 to 700. So within a year and a half post-Bankruptcy, most people have reasonable credit. Usually within two years, the scores will be as though the Bankruptcy never happened.

Chapter 2

What Is Bankruptcy?

Bankruptcy is actually a federal law. That's why it's in the Constitution. The Constitution is quite specific that responsibility for Bankruptcy laws rest with the U.S. Congress, because the framers wanted uniformity in the Bankruptcy laws across the nation. This makes sense: Bankruptcy laws that varied from state to state would make doing business in the United States hopelessly complicated. As a result, with minor variations, Bankruptcy laws are uniform anywhere in the United States.

When we refer to the Bankruptcy laws, we're generally speaking of the Bankruptcy Code. The Bankruptcy Code is Title 11 of the United States Code (a federal law) not to be confused with Chapter 11, which is one chapter of the Bankruptcy Code. Because the Supremacy clause of the Constitution states that federal laws always trump state laws, the Bankruptcy Code is an extremely powerful law. That's what I like about it. Say a creditor sues you and gets a judgment against you. In most cases, Bankruptcy law trumps that judgment. Suppose you signed a contract with someone. In most cases, you can get rid of that contract through Bankruptcy. What if you owe taxes to the IRS? In some cases, you can even get rid of tax debt through Bankruptcy. For people and businesses in financial trouble, there's nothing better.

In addition to the Bankruptcy Code, other laws have bearing on Bankruptcy. Title 18 of the federal code deals with crimes that can be committed while in Bankruptcy. Title 28 deals with the federal court system and includes sections that set up the Bankruptcy Courts and grant these courts certain specific powers under certain specific circumstances.

Specific procedural rules also apply to Bankruptcy Courts. In this book, I'll give you a practical, step-by-step approach to the Chapter 7 Bankruptcy process without bogging you down with a lot of these rules. However, you should know that certain local Bankruptcy Courts have tweaked the laws in one way or another with their own rules. These local rules might change part of the process for you, in your specific locale. With dozens of local courts across the country, I can't discuss each set of local rules. Bear this in mind and check your local laws as you move through the process.

The last set of laws that impact Bankruptcy are your state's laws. While Bankruptcy is a federal law, states can impact that law in two ways. First, even though Congress has the individual power to set up the Bankruptcy process under the Constitution, Congress can delegate certain specific powers to individual state legislatures. One area in particular where Congress has done that is exemptions – an especially complicated and confusing legal concept I'll explore at length in Chapter 10. Congress has made this area a particularly difficult quagmire. Essentially, each state has two sets of exemptions. Some states allow you to use either their local state exemptions or the uniform federal exemptions. In those states, you need to examine each set of exemptions and decide which works better for you. Again, we'll discuss this issue more in Chapter 10. Most states have determined you aren't allowed to pick the federal exemptions. In those states, you can only use state exemptions. In Chapter 10 I'll walk you through this process, but be aware this is one area where Congress delegated its power to the individual states.

The other way state law impacts Bankruptcy is more complex. Bankruptcy is essentially a procedural process through which debtors (you) can assert their legal rights against their creditors (banks, collections firms, people, and companies to whom you owe money). Bankruptcy law, however, doesn't govern the way contracts are read in your state, nor does it address how you own property in your state. It doesn't deal with landlord-tenant law. So while Bankruptcy is a powerful tool, it's still subject to the approach each individual state has taken on those issues and others.

If it seems to you a lot of law governs each Bankruptcy case, then you're right. That's why many attorneys, myself included, specialize in Bankruptcy cases almost exclusively. Generally speaking, I advise people to discuss their cases with an attorney. However, you do have a right to represent yourself in Bankruptcy Court. Many cases that appear before Bankruptcy Court are straightforward and almost mechanical in nature. By following the steps in this book, you can probably navigate the process. However, if your case is more complicated because you run your own business, own multiple pieces of real estate, or have a high income or a lot of assets, you probably should consult a Bankruptcy attorney. If you start representing yourself and a confusing issue comes up, a visit to your local Bankruptcy attorney is warranted. If, like most people, you have limited assets, work for a regular paycheck (or receive Social Security or a pension), and just have a lot of credit card or medical debts, read on.

You should be familiar with certain players in the Bankruptcy process.

Most people are surprised to learn they probably won't ever see a Bankruptcy judge. The person you'll come in contact with is called the trustee. The trustee is usually an attorney appointed by the court to represent your creditors. This is an important fact to bear in mind. Though the trustee may be a nice person, may be pleasant and supportive to you, and may help you through this process, he or she is your opponent. If there's a way to pay back your creditors other than simply giving you a discharge, whether it be through taking some of your property and selling it, whether it be through making you pay back some of your debts going forward, the trustee will play a role in making that happen. So be wary.

The trustee actually doesn't work for the court. He or she is an independent contractor appointed by the local Office of the United States Trustee. The U.S. Trustee's office is an arm of the United States Department of Justice. In short, these guys work for the U.S. Attorney General, and ultimately the President. The people who work in this office are government employees who get paid the same whether you get your discharge or not. They do play an important role in overseeing this process and making sure neither debtors (you) nor creditors (the people and companies to whom you owe money) abuse this process.

The U.S. Trustee's Office looks at a couple of things in particular. First, the people in that office make sure folks who have enough income to pay back their creditors don't file Bankruptcy. To protect against that, the trustee's office may file a motion to dismiss your case. We'll discuss this issue further in Chapter 5.

The other time the U.S. Trustee's Office will pop up is in prosecuting Bankruptcy crimes. The number one rule you need to bear in mind to avoid getting charged with a Bankruptcy crime is: be honest. Don't lie. Don't try to hide things you own. Don't try to put your assets in someone else's name to hide them from creditors. Don't charge up your cards with luxury goods and trips right before you file Bankruptcy. This may seem obvious, but you wouldn't believe the questions people ask me every day. The bottom line is this: you are not more clever than the attorneys, judges, and staff in Bankruptcy Court. There is nothing you can think of that somebody else hasn't already thought of and gotten in trouble for.

By the same token, don't let this scare you off. As long as you're honest, straight-forward, and deal fairly with your creditors and the other parties to your case, you will be fine. In truth, the odds are slim you will ever see anyone from the U.S. Trustee's Office. But if you do, you'll want to get an attorney.

You will certainly come into contact with the Bankruptcy Clerk's office. These offices used to be busy and crowded, staffed with rows of clerks date-stamping document after document. To get served, you stood in a long line behind attorneys and runners pulling wheeled suitcases full of documents to file. That has all changed. A few years ago the courts adopted a system of electronic filing. Attorneys in regular practice before the court are required to file all their documents over the Internet. This procedure saves time and paper. And it made most clerk's offices sleepy back-rooms compared to the past. If you decide to file Bankruptcy on your own, however, you won't have access to this electronic filing system. Therefore, you'll need to go in person to the Bankruptcy clerk's office and hand-file the required documents.

The last issue you need to consider is the fact that you're about to enter an adversarial process – you against your creditors. You are seeking to take property away from them and they won't be happy about it. Despite this fact, you'll find the atmosphere in the courts is non-confrontational. In most districts, a small group of attorneys practice Bankruptcy law. Some represent creditors, some represent trustees, and others are trustees. Some represent debtors like you, and others represent a variety of clients. As a result, we all know and encounter each other time and again. We all fight hard for our clients and always look out for their interests, but we do it in a civilized manner – more so than in most other courts. As a result, you shouldn't go into this process with a chip on your shoulder, ready to fight anyone who stands in your way.

By the same token, be aware that when a trustee or a creditor's attorney is trying to "help" you through the process, they have their own client's interests at heart. Those interests might not be the same as your interests. That is a word for the wise.

At its core, Bankruptcy is a process to help you address your debts. Before you file for Bankruptcy, it's a jungle. Each creditor tries to pound you into submission through phone calls, threatening letters, lawsuits, or garnishments, so that creditor gets paid rather than the others. Each creditor understands you have only so much money, and you can either pay them or another creditor. Believing the squeaky wheel gets the grease, each creditor fights to get its money, not caring whether they hurt you or your other creditors in the process. If you have a number of creditors, you can see how this procedure without Bankruptcy can become chaotic, unpleasant, and downright unfair. In Bankruptcy, we have a process to bring you and all your creditors to the same table, to determine whether you're able to pay any of these creditors, and if so which ones will be paid back and how much. When you look at it this way, you can see Bankruptcy isn't something to aspire to, but in many cases it beats the alternative.

Chapter 3

The Difference Between the Chapters of Bankruptcy

A few years ago, Congress finally passed legislation that was pending for some time. Right before the legislation went into effect in October 2005, the media beat everyone into a frenzy, implying people would no longer be able to file Bankruptcy. In a panic, people who'd been considering Bankruptcy flooded the offices of Bankruptcy attorneys like me to get filed before this law took away the opportunity. I worked long days and nights, helping dozens of people file Bankruptcy before this legislation went into effect. The Bankruptcy Courts were so flooded with filings that the courts were kept open on Saturdays and into the evenings to handle all the cases. Many people who missed that deadline believe they can no longer get a Bankruptcy discharge.

Despite the media hype, most people can still file Chapter 7 Bankruptcy and receive a discharge that wipes out virtually all debts. A few changes in the law were pushing certain high-income individuals into Chapter 13, rather than filing Chapter 7. The changes also require these high-income people to pay back more of their debts than in the past. But most people who could file Chapter 7 Bankruptcy before October 2005 can still file Chapter 7 Bankruptcy and get their discharge.

To clarify this distinction, let's explore the different forms of Bankruptcy.

As stated earlier, all forms of Bankruptcy are created in the federal Bankruptcy Code, Title 11 of the Federal Code of law. Within that Title are a number of Chapters: 1, 3, 5, 7, 9, 11, 12, 13 and 15. Chapters 1, 3, and 5 generally deal with administrative issues. The other chapters deal with kinds of Bankruptcy filings. As a shorthand way to refer to different forms of Bankruptcy filings, we call the filing by the chapter in which it's established. This book is about Chapter 7 Bankruptcy cases, but since you may have read about Chapter 11 cases in the newspaper, and other people may have filed Chapter 13 cases, I'll briefly describe each of these options. I won't go into the other chapters, because they're rarely used and only impact specific kinds of debtors, such as municipal governments (Chapter 9), family farmers and fishermen (Chapter 12), or foreign debtors (Chapter 15).

Chapter 7, of course, is the most common and can be filed by businesses or individuals. The theory behind Chapter 7 Bankruptcy is simple: you get rid of all your debts, you get rid of all your assets, and you get a fresh start. Oftentimes, this chapter of Bankruptcy is referred to as "total Bankruptcy," "real Bankruptcy," and the "fresh start chapter." For a business, that's exactly what happens. The business closes its doors and creditors liquidate whatever is left and distribute it among them.

Congress understood, however, that you can't do that with people. People need to get rid of their debts as a business does, but they need to keep certain assets. People still need a place to live. They require clothing and need a car to get around. What's more, Congress understood that certain assets are more valuable to you than to your creditors. For example, your wedding ring might be worth $1000 to your creditors, but to you it's priceless. Finally, Congress also baked certain policy positions into the Code. For example, Congress wanted people to be able to save for retirement, so it protected your IRAs and 401Ks. Even though the theory of Chapter 7 is that you lose your debts and your assets, most people don't lose anything through this process. We'll discuss this issue further in Chapter 10 and elsewhere.

The discharge is your goal in a Chapter 7 Bankruptcy, and after everything you've gone through, it's rather anti-climactic – often a one-page letter with one sentence saying something to the effect of "it appearing that you are entitled to a discharge, your discharge is hereby granted." Nowadays, letters of discharge aren't even signed by a judge due to electronic filing. Nevertheless, this simple, unassuming letter is one of the most valuable documents you will ever receive.

The discharge is a court order, what we attorneys call an injunction, ordering your creditors to stop trying to collect on your debts. As an order of a federal court it's valid in all fifty states, and even in many other countries. If a creditor violates this court order, that creditor can get into bad trouble, so most creditors are respectful of this order. We'll discuss the discharge more in Chapter 17.

A Chapter 7 case doesn't last long. Most cases take less than five months from start to finish. At the end, once you receive the discharge and your case is closed, you can go on with your life and not have to worry about those debts ever again. That's a good feeling, and it's the reason Chapter 7 is the preferred chapter. This is the chapter I advise most of my clients to file. There are two other forms of Bankruptcy that come up in my office, and each has its time, place, and purpose.

Chapter 13 is the second most common form of Bankruptcy filing. In Chapter 13, you make payments toward your debts for the next three to five years. You may pay 100% of what you owe during this time. You may pay nothing. Or you may pay a small percentage of what you owe.

You may pay no interest to your creditors, or only a low interest rate. What Chapter 13 is all about, however, is paying back something to your creditors. As a result, most creditors like Chapter 13 better than Chapter 7, where they usually get nothing.

Why would someone want to file Chapter 13 and pay back something, rather than just getting rid of their debts? There are two circumstances in which I suggest Chapter 13. First, if a client falls behind on the mortgage payments and wants to keep their home. Typically, if you get behind on your mortgage payments, the bank will insist you mail them the full amount of the arrearage – the "reinstatement amount." I've even seen banks send checks back to my clients if the checks were for less than the full amount. That seems crazy, but it's how banks operate. As a result, if you are a few months behind on your mortgage payment and can't come up with enough money to pay back the full amount of your missed payments, the only way to save your home is through Chapter 13.

What we can do in Chapter 13 is take the amount of the missed payments you owe, the "arrearage," and divide that number by 36 (for three years) or 60 (for five years). Then, in a Chapter 13 case, you can pay back the amount of your missed payments in small increments, typically with no interest. For most people in this situation, that's a far better deal than the mortgage company will offer.

Due to the recent decline in property values, we have a unique opportunity in a Chapter 13 case. During the heady climate of the past few years, mortgage brokers often wrote more than one mortgage on a house. Brokers loved this approach because it resulted in more commissions for them. They sold these mortgages to people who wanted to use the equity in their homes to pay off debts or make certain purchases. They also sold the mortgages to people who didn't have enough money to put down on their home, helping them avoid having to pay PMI mortgage insurance. PMI is a form of insurance many mortgage companies insist on if you don't have at least a twenty percent equity in your home. The theory was, this cushion would protect the mortgage company even if housing prices declined. Without this cushion, the mortgage company wanted insurance to protect against any decline in property values. PMI insurance can be expensive, so clever mortgage brokers realized they could sell you a first mortgage for eighty percent of the value of your home, and then a second mortgage for the remaining twenty percent. The interest rate on the second mortgage would be higher than the interest rate on the first because of the additional risk. But during this era of low interest rates, the payment on that second mortgage was often less than the cost of the PMI insurance – especially when taking the mortgage interest deduction into account. As a result, many people ended up with second mortgages.

With the recent decline in housing values, millions of home owners now owe more on their homes than the homes are worth. In fact, they owe more on just the first mortgage than they could sell their home for. In effect, if the house was sold, there would be only enough equity to pay off the first mortgage. The second mortgage would get nothing, so its lien on the home has no value. It's essentially the same as a credit card, and we lawyers consider it an "unsecured" debt – a debt with no security backing it. If the home owner had enough equity to pay at least part of the second mortgage, it would be considered a "secured" debt, since the loan would be protected by security in the equity of the home.

Interestingly, mortgage companies were the first group to realize this issue was a major problem. At one time, if you fell behind in your second mortgage payments, the mortgage company would foreclose, expecting to get its share of the equity. A few years ago when real estate values started to decline, I noticed mortgage companies with second mortgages weren't foreclosing. Instead, they were suing the debtor, much as a credit card issuer or hospital would sue over a debt.

In Chapter 7 cases, this distinction means nothing. However, in a Chapter 13 case, where there's no equity to provide security to the second mortgage, you can get caught up on your first mortgage payments and treat your second mortgage like a credit card debt or a medical bill, paying only a fraction of what you owe with little, if any, interest. At the end of your Chapter 13 case, in three to five years, the second mortgage will be knocked off your home and you'll only owe your first mortgage going forward. This approach can be a substantial benefit to someone who wants to keep his home.

I also advise clients to file Chapter 13 rather than a Chapter 7 when someone is being torn apart by creditors through lawsuits, garnishments, and other forms of harassment, but for one reason or another they aren't eligible for Chapter 7. There are three main reasons someone would not be eligible for Chapter 7.

1. A person who filed Chapter 7 Bankruptcy within the past eight years isn't eligible to file again until the eighth year has expired. Sometimes people can't wait that long. They may have been rebuilding credit after their last Bankruptcy filing and then lost a job or had a serious illness, a divorce, or some other drop in income. When that happens, Chapter 13 may be the only way to deal with creditors. You're eligible for a Chapter 13 discharge only four years after filing Chapter 7. In fact, you can actually file Chapter 13 the day after your Chapter 7 case is closed. You wouldn't be eligible for your discharge, but you'd benefit from all the other protections a debtor receives in a Bankruptcy case. As a result, if you intend to pay back your creditors one hundred percent of what you

owe them, you can do so over time and without interest by filing Chapter 13 – even before you're eligible to receive the discharge in a Chapter 13 case. Oftentimes, that's a far better deal than you can get any other way.

2. The Means Test is another hindrance to filing Chapter 7 Bankruptcy, and I'll further discuss this in Chapter 5. The Means Test is the key component of the 2005 Bankruptcy Code revision the media were pointing to. The goal of the Means Test was to force higher income people to file Chapter 13 Bankruptcy instead of Chapter 7. In the past, a Bankruptcy Court rarely dismissed a Chapter 7 case because the court believed the debtor could pay something back to his creditors. It was purely a judgment call for the Bankruptcy judges, and they had to find that allowing this debtor to get a Chapter 7 discharge would be a "substantial abuse" of the Bankruptcy process. That is a high standard, and the judges rarely found it to apply. This maddened the creditors. In the rare cases when someone actually did file Chapter 13 rather than Chapter 7 due to high income, the case usually lasted three years and the filer paid next to nothing to the creditors. It turned out, in the old regime, Chapter 13 wasn't much better for creditors than Chapter 7. So the banks went to their buddies in Congress and started lobbying. The 2005 "reform" is the result of their efforts.

The reform made two major changes: the old standard of "substantial abuse" was changed to require that a Chapter 7 case found to "abuse" the Bankruptcy process was either dismissed by the judge or converted to Chapter 13. Purportedly, this was a lower standard and would result in forcing more cases into Chapter 13. The other change was institution of the means test, which examined your total household income over the past six months. If your household income is more than the median household income for a household your size in your state, then you can take certain specific deductions governed by what the IRS considers reasonable in its cases. If you still have more than $100 per month to pay to your creditors, you aren't eligible for Chapter 7 Bankruptcy.

Creditors love this means test. It takes discretion away from Bankruptcy judges the creditors believe were too friendly toward debtors. If you're above the median household income for a family your size in your state, your plan must run for five years. The means test calculates a minimum amount of money that must be paid to your unsecured creditors. This would eliminate Chapter 13 cases for high income debtors who pay nothing or next to nothing on their credit card debt. This is the key provision the banks wanted in the new law.

3. The last reason someone might not be eligible for Chapter 7 Bankruptcy and might instead want to file Chapter 13 is only a quasi-eligibility issue. This issue doesn't bar someone from filing Chapter 7 as the other two reasons do, but from a practical perspective it makes Chapter 7 unattractive. This policy concerns unexempt equity you own. I'll discuss this issue at length in Chapter 10, but it comes down to this: with Chapter 7, you get to keep your property through "exemptions." These exemptions are provisions in the law that allow you to keep certain kinds of property up to a certain value. Generally speaking, exemptions are generous, and most people have no problem keeping all their assets. However, some people have more assets than can be protected. If that's the case, those assets will be taken by the Chapter 7 Trustee and sold. Once the Trustee sells the unprotected, or "nonexempt" asset, he or she takes a cut and distributes the rest on a pro-rata basis to the creditors. For some people with certain high value assets, this prospect might be a deal-breaker, and could make them, for all practical purposes, ineligible for Chapter 7.

But what if they have a lot of debts and creditors are tearing them apart? That's where Chapter 13 can be a useful tool. Creditors in a Chapter 13 case must get at least what they would get in a Chapter 7 case. But the creditors can get that amount over five years, with little to no interest. As long as the debtor does that, he gets to keep nonexempt property. To some people, this is a good solution.

While Chapter 13 may be a good option for someone who's ineligible for Chapter 7, in my experience the number of people who fall into one of those categories is small. Most people are eligible for Chapter 7.

Sometimes, people don't qualify for either option. A business cannot file Chapter 13, only an individual can. Second, you must have a regular source of income. That doesn't mean a job – it could be a pension, Social Security, unemployment compensation, or your own business. But if you have no income, or insufficient income to make the payments in your plan, you can't file Chapter 13. Lastly, there is actually a debt limit to Chapter 13 cases. Chapter 13 is essentially an expedited process for regular people to reorganize their debts. If you have a high amount of debt, like in the millions, Chapter 13 may not be for you.

And that brings us to Chapter 11.

Chapter 11 Bankruptcy is the big daddy of them all. This is the chapter you read about in the newspapers, filed by companies like General Motors and United Airlines. This is the chapter the very rich like Donald Trump's companies file. But it's a complex, expensive process. Chapter 11 makes sense to these companies because it allows them to continue in business – they don't need to shut down. The process lets these businesses and high net worth people reorganize debts so they can make limited payments. Creditors need to get at least as much in Chapter 11 as they'd get in Chapter 7, but you can imagine how important it is to the employees and customers of a company like GM or United Airlines that the company continues operating. Chapter 11 gives them that option.

Here's my best advice: do not attempt to file Chapter 13 or Chapter 11 without a qualified attorney. The good news is that most of the legal fees in a Chapter 13 case can be taken care of as part of your repayment plan. Therefore, many attorneys only require a small down payment to start the process.

As we discussed earlier, however, a person with few legal skills can successfully navigate a relatively simple Chapter 7 case. And that's where this book comes in.

Chapter 4

Why File Bankruptcy?

You'll know when you have to file Bankruptcy. None of my clients have any doubt when the time comes because they're completely overwhelmed by debt and unable to pay.

Signs that Bankruptcy is necessary include lawsuits filed against you and garnishments that impact your bank account, pay checks, or tax refunds. Garnishments are particularly insidious and usually come on the heels of a judgment in a lawsuit. In many states, a creditor can take twenty-five percent of your gross income. Such a dramatic cut in your income can be devastating, resulting in missed mortgage or car payments and lack of funds to pay for such things as groceries, utilities and insurance. A garnishment of your bank accounts can be worse than garnishment of your pay checks. A bank account garnishment is a one-time thing, but it takes everything from your account. If you recently deposited a large paycheck, every cent of it will be taken, no matter what the limits on garnishing your paycheck. What's more, if you wrote checks against that bank account to pay other bills, those checks will bounce, resulting in bank fees and late fees on top of what you already owe.

Certain types of income are protected from most garnishment, including federal tax returns and certain pensions. But once those funds are in your bank account, the creditor can grab them through garnishment. Some creditors find out in advance when you receive payments, such as a Social Security or pension direct deposit, and they time their garnishments to get those funds. This can be devastating.

Creditors also have other tools at their disposal to collect debts. They can have a deputy sheriff go to your home and seize assets. I've had clients lose cars, lawnmowers, or other personal property through this process. They can put a lien on your house, so when you sell it they get paid in full. In rare cases, creditors can even get the court to appoint a receiver to take control of your finances. If you think life was bad when the creditors were calling your home twenty times a day, you haven't seen anything. Fortunately, most of those collection efforts can be undone in Bankruptcy if you file soon enough.

The biggest reason people file Bankruptcy has to do with intangibles. Let me explain.

Financial pressure can lead to extreme emotional distress. I've seen people have heart attacks or commit suicide because of debt. I've seen marriages come apart over the stress of financial pressure. Debt can be ended through Bankruptcy, but heart attacks, suicide, and divorce are forever. When you get to the end of your rope, consider Bankruptcy. There is a way out.

Everyone has a different breaking point. For some people, a single nasty call from a creditor is the limit. Others manage just fine until they start losing a big chunk of their pay to garnishments. I can't tell you when you need to file, but I do believe you'll know when the time comes.

One of the biggest mistakes people make is using money from their IRAs or 401Ks to pay creditors. In Bankruptcy, your retirement savings are fully protected. The only way your creditors can access them is if you hand them over. Congress considers 401Ks and IRAs your funds for retirement. So does your employer. So should you. Those funds should provide security in your old age when you're unable to work. Please, please, do not use these funds to relieve yourself of phone calls from creditors. In the long term, that's a big mistake.

Another mistake I frequently see people make is to pay unsecured debts, such as credit cards, medical bills, and personal loans, rather than their secured debts like mortgages and car loans. Unsecured creditors have no security in anything of yours. To collect from you, they ultimately have to sue you and then pursue garnishments or other collection approaches. Secured creditors have liens on your property. If you miss payments to them, they'll take back the property through foreclosure (in the case of real estate) or repossession, in the case of car loans, boat loans, and the like. Secured creditors usually don't need a court order to take back their property, so if you miss your car payments for a few months, you might leave work to find your car missing. Getting relief from annoying phone calls isn't worth the risk of losing property that helps you survive.

I know Bankruptcy can be scary, but most of my clients tell me, "If only we'd taken this step sooner." Dozens of people came into my office looking tired, worried, and haggard. Married couples are arguing, facing stress in their marriage. When I see them a few months later, they're happier and healthier. Married couples are holding hands again. This is why I enjoy my job as a Bankruptcy attorney. If you're facing this kind of stress, then Bankruptcy might be an option for you.

Chapter 5

Am I Eligible to File Chapter 7 Bankruptcy?

*B*efore we move deeper into this topic, let me give you a few words of encouragement. These forms may seem overwhelming. This book may seem long and detailed. But you can succeed if you follow the process set out in this book one step at a time. Relax and let me walk you through this process.

Now we get into the meat of the procedure. Even though the means test is the last document in the Bankruptcy documents you'll file with the court, you should complete this step first. I've seen people go through the entire Bankruptcy petition and finish dozens of pages, only to reach the last document and find they aren't eligible for Chapter 7 Bankruptcy. In all my cases, this is where I start, and I suggest the same for you.

I've included a blank Bankruptcy petition as Appendix A in this book. However, these documents are constantly changing. I advise you to go to the following website:

http://www.uscourts.gov/bkforms/bankruptcy_forms.html,

where you can download the most current forms. The Chapter 7 Means Test is form B 22A.

Before you begin, you'll need to answer a few more questions. First, have you filed Bankruptcy before? If the answer is yes, then how long ago? If you filed Bankruptcy within the last eight years, put this book away and either wait until the eight years have passed, or visit a Bankruptcy attorney to discuss your other options.

Notice the box on the top right hand side of the Means Test. You'll see three boxes:

- the Presumption arises
- the Presumption does not arise
- the Presumption is temporarily inapplicable

This is Bankruptcy lawyer language. The presumption they're talking about is the presumption of abuse. Essentially, this says if you aren't eligible for Chapter 7 under the Means Test, then your case is presumed to be abusive of the Bankruptcy process. If you are eligible for Chapter 7 under the Means Test, then your case is not presumed to be abusive of the Bankruptcy process. For our purposes here, we'll ignore the third option because I believe it is a big waste of time, space and paper (one of the heights of Congressional idiocy – but that's for another book). The bottom line is this: if you pass the Means Test at any point, check the box that the presumption does not arise; if you fail the Means Test, go see a Bankruptcy attorney to discuss your options. The only good option here is the box that the presumption does not arise, so go ahead and check that box now.

The next step in the process is determining the nature of your debts. If your debts are primarily used for business purposes, then you don't need to do the Means Test. However, that question is a little more complicated than it might seem at first.

First, remember that home mortgages are generally considered consumer debt. So your business debts would have to equal more than the value of your home mortgages. Also, business debts might be in your name. For example, many small business-people, myself included, use personal credit cards to pay business expenses. Or, as a business-person, you may have signed personal guarantees for your business debts. That's because it's nearly impossible for a small business to get financing without the owner signing for the debt also. These debts, even if they're personal debts because they weren't used to finance consumer purchases, are considered non-consumer debts for our purposes.

Also, many people engaged in real estate investing right at the height of the real estate bubble. (It's okay. You didn't have a crystal ball, and you're certainly not alone.) The mortgages on those properties, since they were used for investment purposes and not consumer purposes, are business debts, not consumer debts. If a bare majority of your debts – anything more than 50% of your debts – were used for these types of purposes, then all you do is check 1B, the Declaration of Non-consumer Debts, and sign the last page. You're done. Due to the non-consumer nature of most of your debts, the Means Test does not apply. You have passed the first test as to your eligibility for Chapter 7 Bankruptcy.

The Chapter 7 means test does not apply to one more group of people. If you are a disabled veteran who incurred your debts while you were engaged in active duty or on a "homeland defense activity," then you can check 1A. You are automatically eligible for Chapter 7. Everyone else needs to leave those boxes blank and move on to the next step.

Next, you need to state your marriage status. Are you unmarried, including divorced? Married, and filing jointly? If you're married, you need not file with your spouse, but you may need to take your spouse's income into consideration. Congress was concerned a married couple might be in a situation where one spouse earns all the income and the other has all the debt. They wanted to make sure the one spouse who has all the debt doesn't file Bankruptcy when the other spouse could easily afford to pay the creditors. As a result, you need to take your entire household income into consideration, even if the other spouse isn't filing. There is one exception to that rule. If a married couple is separated or otherwise in a situation where they keep finances and households entirely separate, then you can check "Married not filing jointly, with the declaration of separate households." If you truly maintain separate households from your spouse, then you can check that box and you don't need to include your spouse's income in the calculation. But, in that case, you need to file an additional document called the declaration of separate households. I've included a sample of this document in Appendix D at the end of the book.

Here are your choices:

- Unmarried
- Married not filing jointly, with the declaration of separate households
- Married not filing jointly, without the declaration of separate households
- Married filing jointly

In Chapter 6 we'll discuss whether you should file married jointly or individually. If you know which one to check at this time, mark the correct choice and move on to the next question.

This is the meat of the issue: your income. First you must calculate the average monthly income for you and your spouse (if you have one) for the last full six calendar months. We're talking calendar months here, not actual months. As a result, if you file your case on July 1, the time period you must average is January 1 to June 30. If you file your case on July 31, the time period you must average is also January 1 to June 30. If you get a big bonus on July 2 and you file your case on July 31, the bonus doesn't come into consideration.

There are three ways to calculate your wages over the last six calendar months. The first is to look at your paychecks and add all the gross income amounts from all the checks. Remember, you add the gross, not the net. The gross is before taxes, before insurance and other deductions. The deductions will come into play later, if necessary. The second way only applies if you're on salary and your pay never changes. If that's the case, you can simply take one paycheck and use the following calculation:

How often you're paid	calculation
weekly	gross pay x52÷12
biweekly	gross pay x26÷12

Remember, we're using gross pay figures and not net pay: pre-tax and pre-deductions, not take home pay.

Many people think that if they're paid weekly, they can just multiply their pay by four, since every month has about four weeks. That won't work. Months actually have slightly more than four weeks. The same problem applies if you are paid bi-weekly. Therefore, you need to use the above calculation.

The last option is to do a calculation using the year-to-date gross income listed on your paychecks. The following table illustrates how to do the calculation:

NOTE: ytd stands for year-to-date

If you file in January
use this calculation:

   (ytd of last paycheck in December - ytd of last paycheck in June)÷6
If you file in February
use this calculation:

   (ytd of last paycheck in December - ytd of last paycheck in July + ytd of last paycheck in January)÷6
If you file in March
use this calculation:

   (ytd of last paycheck in December - ytd of last paycheck in August + ytd of last paycheck in February)÷6
If you file in April
use this calculation:

   (ytd of last paycheck in December - ytd of last paycheck in September + ytd of last paycheck in March)÷6
If you file in May
use this calculation:

   (ytd of last paycheck in December - ytd of last paycheck in October + ytd of last paycheck in April)÷6
If you file in June
use this calculation:

   (ytd of last paycheck in December - ytd of last paycheck in November + ytd of last paycheck in May)÷6
If you file in July
use this calculation:

   (ytd last paycheck in June)÷6

If you file in August
use this calculation:

(ytd of last paycheck in July - ytd of last paycheck in January)÷6

If you file in September
use this calculation:

(ytd of last paycheck in August - ytd of last paycheck in February)÷6

If you file in October
use this calculation:

(ytd of last paycheck in September - ytd of last paycheck in March)÷6

If you file in November
use this calculation:

(ytd of last paycheck in October - ytd of last paycheck in April)÷6

If you file in December
use this calculation:

(ytd of last paycheck in November - ytd of last paycheck in May)÷6

You need to do one of the above calculations for each job you and your spouse have. Then you add the average monthly pay for all your jobs and put the sum in Box 3 of Column A. You'll do the same for all your spouse's jobs in Box 3 of Column B.

Line 4 applies only if you're self-employed. If that's the case, then you need bank statements for your business income for the prior six calendar months. If you don't deposit all your business income, estimate it as accurately as you can, and put that on Line 4a for Gross Receipts. Then, you need to determine your business expenses for that same period and put that number on Line 4b as your Business Expenses. Then subtract 4b from 4a and put that in 4c. Place that number in Box 4, Column A if you have the business income, or box 4, Column B if your spouse has the business.

Line 5 applies only if you have rental income. This may be the result of an investment property you own, or rent you receive from a roommate. Complete line 5 the same way you complete line 4.

Line 6 applies only if you receive interest, dividends or royalties. Put that monthly figure for the prior six calendar months in the applicable box and move on.

Line 7 is used by retirees. In that box, place the monthly income you receive from a pension. Do not put Social Security here. For the Means Test, Social Security income isn't considered income. As a result, if your only source of income is Social Security, you have no income and you're done. This box only applies if you receive a pension from a former employer or some other source.

Line 8 applies if you receive child support, alimony, or other domestic support. Here again, Bankruptcy law is different than tax law. While child support income generally isn't considered taxable income, for the Means Test you need to include it. If you receive a monthly payment as a result of a property settlement in a divorce, include that monthly payment as income. All sources of income must be listed, except Social Security, and income that comes from the Social Security Act. That's where Line 9 is a little different. I contend, as do many Bankruptcy attorneys, that unemployment compensation is a benefit under the Social Security Act. As a result, I would place the average monthly unemployment compensation you or your spouse receive in the appropriate box to the left of the columns, and then leave Columns A and B blank. This could make a difference as to whether or not you're eligible for Chapter 7 Bankruptcy.

On Line 10, put other sources of income that don't fit anywhere else.

One more point to clarify – if you started receiving a certain kind of income less than six months ago, then average that amount for six months. For example, if you're filing in July and you received $1000 per month unemployment compensation starting on April 1, then the average is $500 per month monthly income (April, May, June = 3 months x $1000 per month = $3000 ÷ 6 = $500 per month).

Now, add it up. On Line 11, place the totals for each column. On Line 12, put the totals for column A and column B. That's your total current monthly income for the entire household.

On Line 13, take the total from Line 12, multiply that number by 12, and list your average annual income.

On Line 14, you need to determine the applicable median family income for your state. First, list your state in 14a. Second, put your household size in the space at 14b.

Household size is more difficult to calculate than you might think. The standard most frequently cited by Bankruptcy attorneys is "heads on beds." Here's how you calculate it.

If you are married and not separated (i.e. you are not filing the declaration of separate households)
- add 1

If you have children who live with you at least 50% of the time
- add 1 for each child

If you have elderly relatives who you support who live with you
- add 1 for each relative

If you have other relatives who live with you who you support
- add 1 for each relative

If you have a boyfriend/girlfriend who lives with you who you support
- add 1

Again, here Bankruptcy law differs from tax law. For example, if you have a child over 18 whose primary residence is your home, and you support that person, he or she is a dependent under Bankruptcy law, even if not classified as a dependent under tax law.

If an elderly relative is living with you, he or she may qualify as a dependent for the purposes of the Means Test, but that person may also provide you with income under the Means Test. For example, an elderly relative who is your dependent may receive a pension (remember, Social Security income is not income for the Means Test). That pension is therefore part of your household monthly income. The same may be true for a grown child who works, or other relatives who live in your home. What the law gives with one hand, it takes away with the other. Now that you've determined household size, go to the following website:

http://www.justice.gov/ust/eo/bapcpa/20100315/bci_data/median_
income_table.htm.

There, you can look up your state, find the column for the household size, and select the applicable median household income. The table only goes up to a household size of four, so if you have more than four people, you need to add $7500 for each person above four people to the number for four. For example, if you live in Alabama and have a household size of six, the median household income for your family will be $80,079 ($65,079 plus $7500x2). List that number in the box of line 14.

Now comes one of the key tests in this entire process: do you qualify for Chapter 7 Bankruptcy at this time, or do you need to continue through the rest of the Means Test? Line 15 offers a simple test to make that determination. If Line 14 is greater than Line 13, check the first box in line 15, sign the document, and you're done. If Line 13 is larger than Line 14, you still have work to do on the Means Test.

Next is where Congress allows you to take certain deductions to see if you will then qualify for Chapter 7. Remember, don't proceed any further if you've already determined that you qualify.

On line 16, put the total current monthly income from line 12.

Line 17 applies if you're married and living with your spouse, but not filing joint Bankruptcy with your spouse. If this is the case, your spouse may have certain expenses that only help him or her. In short, that portion of your spouse's income doesn't go toward household expenses – including debts that are only in your spouse's name. The monthly payment should be listed there. This could include membership in a club only your spouse belongs to. It might even include your spouse's cigarettes if your spouse smokes. In each case, you should list the type of expense (in the spaces next to a, b, c – you can add additional sheets if needed) and the monthly amount of that expense. Then total these expenses and put that number in the box for line 17.

For line 18, you simply subtract line 17 from line 16 and put that number in line 18.

Next, you must subtract certain specific deductions as determined by the IRS. These numbers change annually, but were current at the time of writing. For updated figures, go to the following website:

http://www.justice.gov/ust/eo/bapcpa/20100315/ meanstesting.htm

For line 19A, use the following figures:

**Bankruptcy Allowable Living Expenses –
National Standards (See 11 U.S.C. § 707(b)(2)(A)(ii)(I))**

Expense	One Person
	Two Persons
	Three Persons
	Four Persons
Food & Clothing (Apparel & Services)*	$371
	$699
	$835
	$996
More than four persons	Additional Amount Per Person
Food & Clothing (Apparel & Services)*	$190

For line 19B, the current figures are as follows:

Under 65	**$60**
65 and Older	**$144**

Note that figures for line 19B are for each person in the household. Therefore, if you have a household with two people over 65 and three people under 65, the line 19B figure would be $468 ($144x2+$60x3).

For line 20A, go to the following website,

http://www.justice.gov/ust/eo/bapcpa/20091101/meanstesting.htm,

go to item 4a on the page, select your state and hit "go." On the page that appears, find your county and household size. The number for "non-mortgage" is what goes in item 20A.

For item 20B, use the same table as 20A. Put the number for "mortgage/rent" for your county and your household size in space **a**. Next, add your monthly mortgage expense. Remember, if you have one mortgage payment, only put that number in space **b**. If you have two or more mortgages, including one that might be a home equity loan, add the monthly payments for all your mortgages and home equity loans and put that number in space **b**. Next, subtract **b** from **a**. If the number is positive, put that number in the box for 20B. If the number is zero or negative, put a zero in the box for 20B.

For item 21, you can adjust the numbers regarding housing expenses if you believe they are inaccurate. The most frequent entry for this box relates to your mortgage. Most people pay property taxes and homeowners' insurance through an escrow account to which they contribute monthly as they make their mortgage payments. If you don't pay your taxes or homeowner's insurance through your mortgage payment, then figure your monthly tax and homeowner's insurance expense and put that number in the box for 21. Then write in the space below the text "taxes and insurance not escrowed." To calculate your monthly tax and insurance expense, add your annual taxes and divide that number by twelve. Do the same for the homeowners' insurance if you do not make that payment monthly. Then total this monthly figure and put it in the box for 21.

Another way to use this box is for dues to a homeowners' association. Again, if you pay monthly dues, put that figure in the box for 21. If you pay annual dues, divide that number by 12 and put the monthly figure in box 21. In the space below the text for 21, write "homeowners' association dues."

Lastly, suppose your rent is more than the number listed in 20B (don't worry if your mortgage payment is more than that number – we'll get to that later). Take the amount of monthly rent you pay and subtract the number in 20B from your rent figure. Put the result of that subtraction in the box for 21, and write "additional rent expense" in the space below the text for 21.

Next we'll address transportation allowances. For 22A, go to the following website,

http://www.justice.gov/ust/eo/bapcpa/20100315/meanstesting.htm.

For item 4b on that page, select your region and hit "go." Next to 22A, check the box indicating whether you own zero vehicles, one vehicle, or two or more vehicles. We are only indicating here how many vehicles you own, not how many you make car payments on. Furthermore, if you're married and filing separately without the declaration of separate households, and you and your spouse each own a vehicle, then you should check the box for 2 or more vehicles. Here we need to know how many vehicles your household owns, because we're looking at household income and expenses. If an adult child who's a dependent of yours owns a vehicle for which you pay the operating expenses, you would take that vehicle into consideration too – even if your name isn't on the title.

For line 22A, check the table that comes up once you've selected your region on the Internet. From that table, select the line that best describes the area in which you live, then pick the number from the column for one vehicle or two vehicles, depending upon which applies. If you do not have a vehicle, put $173 in box 22A to represent public transportation expenses.

Line 22B applies if you live in an area where you use public transportation in addition to owning a vehicle. If that's the case, put $173 in box 22B. If that doesn't apply to you, then move on.

Line 23 is where we deal with the ownership costs of a vehicle. Note that this line applies even if you're leasing a car or truck. Also, remember we're talking about your household owning or leasing vehicles, not just you. If you do not own or lease a vehicle, move on to line 25.

Back to line 23. First check how many vehicles you own or lease. The choices are "one" or "two or more." Then, in the box for 23a, put $489. If you have a car payment that you make, whether it be a lease payment or a loan payment, put that monthly payment in 23b. Subtract 23b from 23a and put the resulting number in the box for line 23. If you have more than one vehicle for which your household pays the ownership expenses, repeat the same process for line 24. If not, let's move on.

Line 25 deals with taxes. For this line, pull out the pay stubs we used to calculate the income for all your jobs and all your spouse's jobs. From the pay stubs, we will now focus on the deductions for taxes: city, state, Federal, Medicare, Social Security, and any other taxes withheld from your pay. To calculate your monthly tax expense, use the same process we used to calculate your pay.

If you're paid on a salary basis and your pay never changes, add all the tax deductions on your paycheck and calculate the monthly tax expense as follows:

How often you're paid	calculation
weekly	Tax deductions x52÷12
biweekly	Tax deductions x26÷12

If you are not paid a salary and your pay changes from one paycheck to the next, then you need to either add and average all the tax deductions from your paychecks over the last six calendar months, or use the year-to-date approach as follows:

If you file in January
use this calculation:

(ytd of last paycheck in December - ytd of last paycheck in June)÷6

If you file in February
use this calculation:

(ytd of last paycheck in December - ytd of last paycheck in July + ytd of last paycheck in January)÷6

If you file in March
use this calculation:

(ytd of last paycheck in December - ytd of last paycheck in August + ytd of last paycheck in February)÷6

If you file in April
use this calculation:

(ytd of last paycheck in December - ytd of last paycheck in September + ytd of last paycheck in March)÷6

If you file in May
use this calculation:

(ytd of last paycheck in December - ytd of last paycheck in October + ytd of last paycheck in April)÷6

If you file in June
use this calculation:

(ytd of last paycheck in December - ytd of last paycheck in November + ytd of last paycheck in May)÷6

If you file in July
use this calculation:

(ytd last paycheck in June)÷6

If you file in August
use this calculation:

(ytd of last paycheck in July - ytd of last paycheck in January)÷6

If you file in September
use this calculation:

(ytd of last paycheck in August - ytd of last paycheck in February)÷6

If you file in October
use this calculation:

(ytd of last paycheck in September - ytd of last paycheck in March)÷6

If you file in November
use this calculation:

(ytd of last paycheck in October - ytd of last paycheck in April)÷6

If you file in December
use this calculation:

(ytd of last paycheck in November - ytd of last paycheck in May)÷6

Remember to add the taxes for all your jobs and all your spouse's jobs, plus any other jobs that contribute to the household income. If a pension comes into the household income and taxes are withheld from that, add the monthly amount withheld for taxes. If you or your spouse are self-employed, you need to work with your accountant to determine your monthly tax expense.

Lastly, if you owe taxes at the end of the year rather than receiving a refund, take the amount you owe from both your federal and state returns, divide that amount by 12, and add that amount to the total sum of all the income taxes you pay. Once you've totaled that number, put it in box 25.

Keep the paycheck stubs in front of you. We aren't finished with them yet. For line 26, look at your paycheck stubs for any of the following deductions: union dues, uniform, mandatory pension deduction (note – this does not include a 401K deduction if that is voluntary), and, in my opinion, the payment on a 401K loan should apply here as well. Note that insurance deductions or any voluntary deductions should not be considered here. Look at all the paychecks for each member of your household and add those deductions. Determine the monthly expense for all those expenses and put that number in box 26.

Line 27 deals with life insurance. This payment could be life insurance you pay for through work, or pay directly. This is one place where general household expenses don't matter. Only life insurance for you and your spouse (if filing jointly) matters here. Furthermore, we're only dealing with term life insurance. Disability insurance doesn't apply. Neither does a whole life or cash value life insurance policy you can borrow from. This expense doesn't need to be averaged the past six full calendar months. Instead, list what you are currently paying for term life insurance. Add that figure and put it in the box for line 27.

Line 28 is for alimony or child support payments you're required to make, either directly or through a state agency. It doesn't matter if payments are withheld from your paycheck or you send a check. If the amount is court ordered, you can include this monthly expense. Put that number in line 28.

Line 29 can include one of two different kinds of expense. If your employer requires you to take classes or continuing education, that expense goes here. If you're simply taking classes in hopes of getting a new job or a promotion, that expense doesn't apply. The form is clear about the fact that the educational expense must be a condition of your employment. On the other hand, if you have a child who is mentally or physically disabled, the monthly expenses you incur to take care of that child also go here. Either way, figure any monthly expense you have in either of these categories and list that number in the box for line 29.

Then move on.

Line 30 deals with childcare expenses. If you have small children, you'll probably need to fill in this line. Obviously the expense for childcare for while you're at work goes here. And the form also allows expenses for babysitting and childcare. So if you pay a babysitter to watch your children on occasion, add that monthly expense. If you have a relative care for your children, any expenses related to that should be factored in here too. The bottom line is: add all your costs for someone else to watch your children, and put that monthly expense in line 30. Take note, however, that educational expenses such as tuition don't go here. We'll get to that expense later.

Line 31 deals with out of pocket expenses for health care. This is a household expense and includes all healthcare expenses for you, your spouse, and all dependents. We aren't talking about health insurance costs or a health savings account. We'll get to those later. Here we're dealing with prescriptions, co-pays, and other out-of-pocket expenses for health care, dental care, eye care, etc. It might be helpful to add your expenses in this category for the last six months and divide that number by six. Put the resulting number in the box for line 31.

Line 32 is for telecommunication expenses other than your cell phone bill and basic home phone bill. If you have a pager, Internet access, call waiting, caller ID, or special long-distance service total those monthly expenses and list that number here.

For line 33, add all the numbers listed in the boxes for lines 19 through 32. Place that number in the box for line 33.

On Line 34, we deal with health insurance. Again, check your paycheck stubs and look for any health insurance deductions on any of your paychecks, your spouse's paychecks, or the checks of any other person who contributes to the household income. Pension checks may also have a health insurance deduction. Remember that health insurance may include dental and vision insurance. Add all these expenses and figure your monthly health insurance expense using the following table:

How often you're paid	calculation
weekly	Health insurance deductions x52÷12
biweekly	Health insurance deductions x26÷12

If you're self-employed, unemployed, or for some other reason directly pay for your health insurance or COBRA, determine your monthly payment for that.

Once you've determined your total monthly household expense for health insurance, place that number in box 34a.

Next, do the same for disability insurance. You may have short-term disability insurance, long-term disability insurance, AFLAC, or another plan. For any such expense you need to determine your monthly total and put that number in box 34b.

Lastly, determine if you have a health savings account. This type of account may be referred to as part of a cafeteria plan, and you'll typically have it through your employer. Such an account deposits pre-tax funds into a special segregated fund. Then, as out-of-pocket health care expenses arise, you pay those bills from the account. In most cases, you lose the funds in the account if you don't use them over the course of the year. Health care expenses you listed in line 31 should be separate from expenses paid out of the health savings account – you don't want to double-count that expense. If you have that expense, calculate the monthly cost based upon the following table, then put that number in the box for 34c.

How often you're paid	calculation
weekly	Health savings deductions x52÷12
biweekly	Health savings deductions x26÷12

Now, add the numbers in boxes 34a, 34b and 34c. Place that sum in the box for line 34.

Line 35 applies if you help support an elderly, chronically ill, or disabled family member. If that's the case, put the average monthly figure for that expense in line 35.

Lines 36 and 37 are rarely used, and quite frankly, you should have an attorney assist you if either of them apply.

On line 38, list educational expenses for your children. To be entered here, the child must be a dependent under the age of 18. Your monthly expense entered here cannot exceed $137.50 per child. This is where you would list private school tuition or other extraordinary educational expenses for your children. Be prepared to provide documentation to support this expense. If this line applies, enter that number – again amounting to no more than $137.50 per child – then move on.

For line 39, use the following table:

Expense	1 Person	2 Persons	3 Persons	3 Persons
5% of Food & Clothing	$19	$35	$42	$50

More than four persons	Additional Amount Per Person
5% of Food & Clothing	$10

Line 40 applies if you make charitable contributions. Any contributions to a church would be entered here, even if you just put cash in the basket and don't have any documentation to support that expense. Divide annual contributions to charities by 12 and enter that figure here. Some employers have deductions for the United Way or another charity. Those deductions should be calculated on a monthly basis using the following table:

How often you're paid	calculation
weekly	charitable deductions x52÷12
biweekly	charitable deductions x26÷12

Add all the monthly charitable contributions made by all members of your household. That monthly number should be listed in the box for line 40.

In line 41, place the sum of all numbers entered for lines 34 to 40.

Next we will deal with certain specified expenses. Earlier, when we calculated the ownership expense for vehicles and your home, we subtracted from that number the payments made on mortgages, car loans and car leases. This is where we add those expenses back into the mix.

On line 42, you'll see a box with lines a, b, and c. This is where we will deal with secured debts such as mortgages, car loans, home equity loans, boat loans, camper loans, and any other type of loan where the creditor has a lien on something you own (essentially an ownership interest that allows the creditor to take back – i.e. repossess or foreclose on – a specific piece of property).

For each line, enter the name of the creditor, the property on which the creditor has a lien, your monthly payment, and whether the payment includes taxes or insurance. There is one issue to note here: if the loan will be paid off in less than 5 years, then you don't enter the actual monthly payment. Instead, you multiply the monthly payment by the number of payments you have remaining. Then, you divide that number by 60 and place that number in the average monthly payment for loans of that type. The formula is as follows:

Formula to calculate the average monthly payment for line 42
for loans that will be paid off in less than 5 years:

monthly payment on the loan
x number of monthly payments remaining ÷60

Here is an example of how the table in line 42 should look when completed:

	Name of Creditor	Property Securing the Debt	Average Monthly Payment	Does payment include taxes or insurance?
a.	CitiMortgage	home	$1,100	X yes _ no
b.	Bank of America	home	$200	_ yes X no
c.	GMAC	Pontiac	$300	_ yes X no
			Total: Add Lines a, b, and c.	

You would add the monthly payments and put the total in the box for line 42. In this case, the number would be $1600 ($1100+$200+$300). Note that if you have more secured creditors than will fit in the box, you can add an additional page.

Line 43 becomes an issue if you have secured loans from line 42 and you're behind in the payments. In that case, for each secured creditor from line 42 for which you're behind, you need to complete a line in the table in line 43. For each line, list the creditor, the property securing the debt, and the amount you're behind on your payments divided by 60. Suppose you're three months ($600) behind in your home equity loan payments to Bank of America. If that's the case, complete line a in the table as follows:

a.	Bank of America	home	$10

Once you've added the creditors from line 42 where you're behind in your payments to the table in line 43, add all the dollar figures and list that number in the box for line 43.

Line 44 applies if you're behind on taxes, alimony, or child support payments. If so, add all the amounts you owe in taxes, alimony, and child support, divide that number by 60, and put the total in the box for line 44. Only include payments you're behind in – do not include on-going obligations for taxes, alimony, or child support. As you may remember, we listed those obligations elsewhere.

Next, add the administrative expenses you would incur if you had to file a Chapter 13 case. This is how you make the calculation: First, add the numbers from the boxes in lines 42 to 44. Place that number in the box for 45a. Next, go to the following website,

http://www.justice.gov/ust/eo/bapcpa/20100315/bci_
data/ch13_exp_mult.htm

and find your state and judicial district. If you don't know your judicial district, you can find it by going to this website,

http://www.justice.gov/ust/eo/bapcpa/ccde/states.htm,

selecting your state then finding your county. Each judicial district will have its own multiplier. Select your judicial district's multiplier and put that number in 45b. Then, multiply the number in 45a by the number in 45b and divide by 100. The resulting number will go in the main box for line 45.

Formula to calculate the number for line 45:
45a x 45b ÷100

Now add the numbers listed in the boxes for lines 42 through 45 and put the resulting total in the box for line 46.

You're almost done.

For line 47, add the totals in the boxes in lines 33, 41 and 46. Put the resulting number in the box for line 47.

In the box for line 48, list the number from the box for line 18.

In the box for line 49, place the number we just calculated for line 47.

Next subtract line 49 from line 48. Place the resulting number in line 50. It's okay if this is a negative number (less than zero).

Now, multiply the number in line 50 by 60 and list that result in the box for line 51.

Formula to calculate the number for line 50:
result in line 50 x 60

Line 52 is another of those determination spaces. Here, you look at the number in line 51. If that number is less than $6,575, you're done. You do qualify for Chapter 7 Bankruptcy. Simply check the first box in line 52, sign the document, and go to the next chapter of this book.

If the number in line 51 is more than $10,950, you're also done. That's the good news. The bad news is, you don't qualify for Chapter 7 Bankruptcy. I advise you to put away this book and set up an appointment with a qualified Bankruptcy attorney.

Lastly, if the number in line 51 is more than $6,575 and less than $10,950, then you must check the third box in line 52 and continue.

If you're still working on this, don't worry, we're nearing the end.

For line 53, you need to add the amount you owe on all your credit cards, personal loans, and medical bills. That number will go in the box for line 53.

For line 54, take the number in line 53 and divide it by 25.

Now comes the final determination. Compare the number in the boxes in line 51 and line 54. If the number on line 54 is larger, congratulations: you qualify for Chapter 7. Check the first box, sign the document, and go to the next chapter of this book.

Unfortunately, if line 51 is larger, this is basically the end of the road for you in Chapter 7. I suggest you meet with a qualified Bankruptcy attorney to discuss your options.

That's it. You've completed the Means Test. Hopefully you qualify for Chapter 7, because after we consider a few more issues we'll get to the meat of filling out the Chapter 7 petition.

Chapter 6

Can I File On My Own If I'm Married?

The short answer is yes, you can file Chapter 7 Bankruptcy on your own if you're married. A better question is – should you?

Despite what some attorneys claim, it costs no more money to file jointly with your spouse than to file individually. Congress specifically set up the Bankruptcy Code to allow for joint filing by married couples. A joint filing takes the same amount of paperwork, time, and effort, as an individual filing, and the filing fees are exactly the same. However, I rarely advise a client to file Bankruptcy without his or her spouse.

In fact, I usually suggest a married couple go forward with a joint filing, even if they're contemplating divorce. Let me explain. When you get divorced, you need to determine how to deal with debts held between the two of you. If you have three joint credit cards, in the divorce decree the court will determine who's responsible for paying each card after the divorce. Once that determination is entered in the divorce decree, it becomes a debt that cannot be discharged through Bankruptcy. In other words, after a divorce decree you'll be locked into paying debts you could've discharged through Bankruptcy.

In such cases, both spouses often end up with debts they won't be able to pay once the divorce is finalized, and neither spouse can get rid of these debts through Bankruptcy. By filing jointly prior to the divorce, the couple can get rid of all their joint debts. None of the discharged debts will be addressed in the divorce decree, and neither spouse has to pay them.

I've had married clients tell me they want to file individually so the credit of the other spouse will be protected. I can tell you that nine times out of ten when a client insists on taking this approach, the spouse is in my office within a year to file Bankruptcy as well. By filing as I usually suggest, they would have saved fifty percent of the fees and costs they ultimately paid.

If you do choose to file individually, the non-filing spouse is not impacted by the Bankruptcy. Even though you need to include your spouse's income and expenses as part of the means test and budget calculations, his name and Social Security number aren't on the forms, so his credit remains unaffected. Theoretically, if all the debts are in your name and not in your spouse's name, such an approach might make sense. But this concept is based upon flawed logic.

First, when one spouse tells me all the debts are in his name with none in the spouse's name, I'm skeptical. Sometimes, without thinking, one spouse adds the other as an authorized user of a credit card. Once the second spouse uses the card, she may also become fully liable for the debt. When you file Bankruptcy, the debt will be discharged against you, but your creditors will attempt to collect from your spouse once your case is over. You'll soon find yourself in the same situation you were in before you filed Bankruptcy.

What's more, even when the debts are completely separated between spouses, each spouse usually has enough debt to make joint Bankruptcy the best option. Suppose one spouse owes $30,000 and the other owes only $5000. The clients may tell me the one with $30,000 in debt wants to file, while keeping the one with $5000 of debt out of it. But when you consider the fact that you pay no more to file jointly than to file individually, it makes sense to get rid of the $5000 as well. Essentially, you'll be getting rid of that debt for free.

The other misconception is believing it makes sense to protect one spouse's credit. The single biggest surprise for most of my clients who go through Bankruptcy is how fast their credit bounces back. If you're relatively current on your debts before filing and follow the strategies in Chapter 20 of this book, within a year your credit will probably reach the high six hundreds. That's not bad. It might even be better than your credit right now. You'll start receiving offers to finance vehicles and for new credit cards shortly after your case is over. Initially, those offers won't be that great, but over time they'll improve.

The point is, given how soon your credit bounces back, it's better to get rid of all debt than try and protect your spouse's credit rating. However, if you do elect to file Bankruptcy on your own, you can do so without impacting your spouse.

Chapter 7

What Debts Can Be Discharged?

*U*nfortunately, not all debts can be discharged in Bankruptcy. Congress boiled certain exceptions to discharge into the code. Some of these exceptions make sense, while others are the result of furious lobbying by special interest groups. The list of non-dischargeable debts has grown over the years. The bottom line is, for some people Chapter 7 Bankruptcy isn't the solution they were hoping for.

Here's the rule: all debts are dischargeable, unless you and your creditor want to keep the debt going, or unless the Bankruptcy Code specifically states this specific kind of debt will not be discharged. Three categories of debt are non-dischargeable:

- First are the debts you want to keep for one reason or another.
- Second are debts that are non-dischargeable.
- Last are debts that are only non-dischargeable if the court specifically orders this.

Perhaps it seems odd to keep debts, but it does happen. What about your car loan or car lease? If you don't keep paying that debt, your vehicle will be repossessed and you won't have transportation. How about mortgages on your home, or your property taxes? If you don't keep paying those debts, your home will be foreclosed upon and you will end up on the streets. I've seen people want to keep a long-term membership with a credit union going. The procedure to keep these debts is called a "reaffirmation agreement." We will discuss this issue more in Chapter 15, but suffice it to say you may want to keep debts that allow you to retain certain property. These debts are voluntarily non-discharged.

Now we come to debts that are automatically non-dischargeable. The most common example is a student loan. Wrongly, in my opinion, student loans and any educational debts are non-dischargeable. Even if you can't afford to pay them now, those debts are virtually impossible to get rid of – even if the debt was incurred so someone else could go to college. Even if the loans were made by a private entity without a governmental guarantee. It doesn't matter. You can't get rid of these debts.

The second most common example of a non-dischargeable debt is a tax debt. Older tax debts for which you filed returns more than three years ago may be discharged. But newer tax debts incurred within the last three years are protected from discharge. Apparently Congress wants to make sure it gets paid.

Another common exception to discharge involves alimony, child support, or other domestic support obligations. Certain debts created in a divorce decree were once dischargeable. But in the reform legislation of 2005, those exceptions were wiped out. At this point, any debt established as a result of a divorce, for child support, or for other domestic support will probably be non-dischargeable. Other important exceptions to discharge include:

- If you live in a condominium and pay association dues, all dues owed before filing Bankruptcy will be discharged. However, you still owe any dues that become current after the Bankruptcy. This can be a problem if you plan to give the condominium back to the bank, because banks sometimes take awhile to complete the process and take the property back. During the period while you're waiting for the bank to take action, you still have to pay the association dues, even if you no longer live there.
- If you don't list a creditor on your petition and don't give them notice of your Bankruptcy before it's closed, that debt might not be discharged.
- If you owe money to repay a 401K loan, you will probably have to continue making those payments. This isn't such a bad thing, because this debt is essentially a debt owed to you. There's a lot to be said for rebuilding your 401K.

Lastly, we consider debts the creditor must take action on to make non-dischargeable. We'll discuss litigation in the Bankruptcy Court in greater detail in Chapter 18, but to make these debts non-dischargeable, the creditor will actually have to sue you and get a judgment on the matter from the court. These debts typically involve some kind of dishonesty or fraud on your part. If you're a straight-shooter, you have nothing to worry about. But you may have a problem...

- If you took a large cash advance or made unusually large charges on a credit card within six months before filing Bankruptcy, you will probably get sued by a creditor to stop this debt from being discharged.
- If you used a credit card or a personal loan to pay taxes, that debt will likely result in a non-dischargeability action.
- If you somehow committed fraud or took money from someone, the liability for that debt will probably result in a non-dischargeability action.

If issues like these are in your past, you should speak with an experienced Bankruptcy attorney. Handling litigation in the Bankruptcy court is not for non-lawyers, or even attorneys with limited experience in Bankruptcy. That's why you need to know what debts might cause problems for you in a Bankruptcy case.

Which debts are discharged in Bankruptcy? Here is a partial list of debts your Bankruptcy can relieve you from...

- credit card debt
- personal loans
- legal judgments – as long as they don't claim some kind of fraud.
- Medical bills
- Collection accounts
- Deficiency balances – These are debts that result when a vehicle, boat, or some other property is repossessed or returned. Losing the property doesn't necessarily wipe out your debt. The deficiency is the difference between what you owe and what the creditor sells the property for. You should note that foreclosed mortgages can also result in deficiency balances creditors try to collect upon. But again, filing Bankruptcy would discharge that debt as well.
- Older tax debts

This is a partial list. The point is, for most people the debts that cause problems are dischargeable in Bankruptcy. However, for some people Bankruptcy isn't a good option. Consider this list as you decide whether Bankruptcy is the best solution to your problems.

Chapter 8

The Credit Counseling Requirements

Many clients who come to my office have heard they need to take classes before they can file Bankruptcy. When the law changed in 2005, a new requirement for credit counseling was added, but you won't be expected to attend a class like in high school or college. The truth is, this requirement is no big deal and you shouldn't be afraid of it.

The class is an important part of the process, although it's relatively easy to complete. If you haven't completed pre-Bankruptcy credit counseling, your case will be dismissed. It doesn't matter if you plan to do it later, it doesn't matter if you meant to do it, it doesn't even matter if you already did it, but not until after you filed. If you don't take care of credit counseling before filing, your case will be dismissed and you'll be back at ground zero.

If you and your spouse are filing jointly, you each need a credit counseling certificate. Most credit counseling companies allow you to do the credit counseling together, but if you use one of those companies, you should enter the information for both spouses and make sure you each get a certificate. If you don't have two certificates, the case will be dismissed for the spouse who didn't get one.

What's more, certain courts have ruled it isn't enough to do the credit counseling before you file: you actually need to do it at least a day before filing. Therefore, this takes a little advance planning. You can't do the credit counseling, then walk your petition into the clerk's office the same day. Although it may seem absurd, you need to get the counseling done at least a day before you file.

Furthermore, your certificate for completing the credit counseling is only valid for six months. As a result, you need to do the first credit counseling within the six months before you file your Bankruptcy case. Again, if you don't comply, your case will be dismissed.

Credit counseling itself is a no big deal, but any old credit counseling company won't work. You need to do the specific pre-bankruptcy credit counseling with a company approved by the U.S. Trustee. For a current list, go to

http://www.justice.gov/ust/eo/bapcpa/ccde/cc_approved.htm

and select your state. Not every company is approved to work in every district, so choose a company that's authorized to offer credit counseling in your judicial district. Again, to determine what district you live in, visit

http://www.justice.gov/ust/eo/bapcpa/ccde/states.htm

and select your state.

Most credit counseling companies offer an on-line program that provides information about different kinds of Bankruptcy, as well as other alternatives to handling your debts. The program will ask you to create a budget and ask for information about your debts and assets. The program will also give you basic information about how to manage your finances. Some of my clients find these programs a gigantic waste of time, while others find them helpful. However, it doesn't matter how you feel – Congress says you have to do it.

The cost for these programs is typically $30 to $50. If they want to charge you more, go to another provider. The process should take one to two hours. If it takes more than two hours, you're working too hard. Know this credit counseling information is not included in your Bankruptcy filing. You just need to complete the counseling and get the certificate. The certificate itself is filed with the court when you file your petition.

Typically, these on-line programs will have some step involved to ensure you're actually following the procedures. I've seen programs require an on-line chat at various steps in the process. Others require you to make a quick phone call to the company after you complete the counseling. Either way, this requirement doesn't add a lot to the process.

If you don't have Internet access or you aren't comfortable on the computer, some programs offer on-site or telephone classes. Shop around to find a company that fits your needs. Some companies are better than others, and some are less expensive. However you do it, complete the counseling and get your certificate.

Once you've filed your case, you still aren't finished. You need to fulfill a second credit counseling requirement within 45 days of your court hearing, or your case will be dismissed and you will not get your discharge. I suggest you take care of this as soon as your case is filed.

To do the second credit counseling, you'll probably return to the same company you already used. Again, you can typically complete this requirement over the Internet, by phone, or in a class. The course should cost from $30 to $50, and should take no more than two hours. This program takes less information from you, but requires more reading. They give you a path forward, with advice on how to avoid getting into money problems in the future. Again, some of my clients find this helpful and some don't, but either way, you have to do it. If you don't like it, write your Congressman. I did, and you can see how much that helped.

Chapter 9

The Petition and Schedules

$\mathcal{T}$his is where the rubber hits the road – where we begin filling in the forms. I will walk you step-by-step through this process.

1. Go to the following website

    http://www.uscourts.gov/bkforms/bankruptcy_forms.html.

    Here you'll find the the forms you need to download. By using a recent version of Adobe Acrobat Reader (available at http://get.adobe.com/reader), you can complete the forms on-line. Otherwise, print them and fill them out by hand.

2. The first form we will deal with is the voluntary petition – form B1.

3. Follow with me step-by-step. First, enter your full legal name – last, first, middle – for example: Greiner, Michael Anthony. If your legal name includes a suffix, such as Jr. or III, be sure you include that.

4. If you're filing a joint petition with your spouse, list his or her name in the space to the right. It doesn't matter which spouse is listed first here. The important thing is be consistent whenever you write your names throughout the documents.

5. Next is a space for you to enter any other legal names you've had in the last eight years. Don't worry about nicknames or misspellings of your actual legal name. The things you'll enter here are former names you changed, maiden names, prior married names, and "doing business as" names, otherwise known as "trade names." For former legal names, you will put the initials f/k/a before the name, signifying "formerly known as." For other legal names by which you're currently known, put the initials a/k/a before the name, signifying "also known as." For legal trade names or doing business as names, put the initials d/b/a for "doing business as," or f/d/b/a for "formerly doing business as."

6. Complete the same process as in 5 for your spouse, if he or she had any other legal names in the last eight years.

7. Next, list your Social Security number on the left and your spouse's Social Security number (if this is a joint filing) on the right.

8. Next you need to put your street address. No P.O. boxes here – this is where you live. Note the zip code goes in the little box to the right.

9. If this is a joint filing, repeat the same step as 8 on the right. You need to do this even if your spouse's address is the same as yours.

10. Next, list the county where you live. This is critical, because it determines which court you'll be assigned to.

11. Again, if this is a joint petition, write your spouse's county on the right even if it's the same as yours.

12. If you have a different mailing address, such as a PO box or a relative's address, write that address next. Again, the zip code goes in the little box to the right. You only need to fill in this line if you have a mailing address different from your street address. Otherwise, leave it blank.

13. If this is a joint petition and your spouse has her own mailing address, put that information in the box to the right, repeating the step from step 12.

14. Skip the box that asks for the "Location of Principal Assets." This box is only used in business cases.

15. Next, under "Type of Debtor," check Individual.

16. The next box you go to is on the right: Chapter of Bankruptcy Code Under Which the Petition is Filed. Under that box, check Chapter 7.

17. Next comes the box Nature of Debts. You may recall when we were determining if you were eligible for Chapter 7 Bankruptcy in Chapter 5 of this book, you filled out the means test to determine whether your debts were mostly of a business nature or not. If your debts were primarily business debts, check the appropriate box. If your debts were not primarily business debts, check the box that says "Debts are primarily consumer debts."

18. Next comes the box Filing Fee. The fee to file a Chapter 7 Bankruptcy case with the court is $299. You have three options in handling that:
     ♦ You can pay the filing fee in full when you file the petition with the court.
     ♦ You can file an application with the court to pay the fee in installments. This requires you to show the court you're financially unable to pay this fee all at once. It is the judge's discretion whether he or she will allow this. We'll further discuss this step in Chapter 12 of this book. If you don't make the payments as required, your case could be dismissed.

♦ You can file an application with the court to waive your filing fee. Again, this option requires you to show the court you cannot afford this payment. The judge can either allow or not allow this. We'll further discuss this option in Chapter 12.

19.　When you decide which of the three options in 18 to choose, check that box under Filing Fee.

20.　Skip the box on Chapter 11 Debtors.

21.　At the bottom of the page, under Statistical/Administrative Information, check the second box saying "Debtor estimates that, after any exempt property is excluded and administrative expenses paid, there will be no funds available."

22.　Under that box, under Estimated Number of Creditors, check box 1-49, unless you have 50 or more creditors. If you have a large number of creditors, check the box that applies.

23.　Under that box, under Estimated Assets, estimate the total value of everything you own. Remember this is garage sale value – a low valuation. This estimate should include the value of your home, car, and 401Ks/IRAs. Check the applicable box.

24.　Under that box, under Estimated Liabilities, estimate the total value of your debts. This estimate should include your mortgage, car loan, credit cards, taxes owed, etc. Once you've determined that estimate, check the correct box.

25.　Go to the next page.

26.　On the top right of the page, under Name of Debtor(s), write your name. If this is a joint petition, write your spouse's name.

27.　Skip down to Exhibit D.

28.　Check the first box.

29.　If this is a joint filing, check the second box as well.

30.　Skip to the next box, Information Regarding the Debtor – Venue.

31.　Check the first box there.

32.　If your landlord has a judgment evicting you from your home, you might want to talk to a qualified Bankruptcy attorney as soon as possible. If not, go to the next page.

33.　 Go to Appendix B in this book and read that document.

34.　On the top right of the page, under Name of Debtor(s), write your name. If this is a joint petition, add your spouse's name.

35.　On the top left of the page you'll see a box that says Signature(s) of Debtor(s) (Individual/Joint). Read the text at the top of that box. This is the most important of all your signatures. Your signature certifies you understand that you're completing this petition under penalty of perjury, and that you need to tell the truth. You're also stating you understand that you can file under any of the chapters of Bankruptcy, but you've chosen to file Chapter 7. Lastly, you're stating you have read the document in Appendix B of this book.

36.   Sign at the X under that text.

37.   If you're doing a joint filing, have your spouse sign next to the second X.

38.   Below that, write your phone number, including your area code.

39.   Below that, write the date.

40.   You have now completed the petition and we'll move to the next document.

41.   Go back to the following website

http://www.uscourts.gov/bkforms/bankruptcy_forms.html.

In the same area where you found the petition, under B1, you will see Exhibit D. That is what we'll work on next.

42.   On the top left of the page, next to "In re" write your name and, if this is a joint petition, add your spouse's name.

43.   Check box number 1.

44.   Sign and date the document on the second page.

45.   Attach your credit counseling certificate to this document.

46.   If you're filing jointly, you need to print a second Exhibit D for your spouse to sign, then attach the credit counseling certificate for your spouse to that document. In other words, if filing jointly, you'll have two copies of Exhibit D signed separately by each spouse.

47.   Next, return to the following website:

http://www.uscourts.gov/bkforms/bankruptcy_forms.html.

There you will open up B6A – Schedule A – Real Property.

48.   On the top left of the page, next to In re, write your name. If this is a joint petition, add your spouse's name.

49.   Real property is what we attorneys call real estate. On this page, list any real estate you own. This includes your home if you own it, plus any other real estate, even if you owe money on it (a mortgage and/or home equity loan and/or property taxes). If you're listed on a relative's home, you need to list it here as well. Don't list your home if you are renting.

50.   In the column to the left, describe the property as follows:
    ♦ If it's your home, write *debtor's homestead*
    ♦ If it's rental property or other investment property, write *investment property*.
    ♦ If it's a vacation home, write *vacation property*.
    ♦ If it's vacant property, write *vacant property*.

51.   Below the description of the property, write the address of that property.

52. In the second column, write as follows:
    ♦ If you own the real estate, even if you have a mortgage or home equity loan on it, you will write *Fee Simple*.
    ♦ If you have any kind of other ownership of any real estate, I strongly advise you to speak with an attorney.
53. In the third column, write as follows:
    ♦ If you (the husband) are the only one with your name on the property's deed, you will write H.
    ♦ If you (the wife) are the only one with your name on the property's deed, you will write W.
    ♦ If you're married and own the property jointly with your spouse, even if you aren't filing this case jointly, write J.
    ♦ If you own the property along with anyone else, write J.
    ♦ If you're married and live in one of the following states, you will write C:
    - Alaska
    - Arizona
    - California
    - Idaho
    - Louisiana
    - Nevada
    - New Mexico
    - Puerto Rico
    - Texas
    - Washington
    - Wisconsin
54. In the fourth column, list the value of your property. Remember, you want to value this property low, as though you had to sell it in an emergency. Ideally, you'll have a recent appraisal or tax bill that tells you what your local assessor thinks the property is worth. But that value may not be the end of the story. Especially in the current economy, an appraisal of even a few months ago might dramatically overstate value of the real estate. Assessors have typically been slow to respond to this crisis. As a result, if you believe your property is worth less than the appraisal or assessment, list your estimated figure on this form. However, be prepared to defend your estimate if it's different. Everyone in the Bankruptcy Court knows how this economy has affected real estate values, so they'll understand where you're coming from. Last but not least, if you own this property jointly with one or more people, you need to divide the overall value by the number of people with whom you own the property. For example, if you and your wife are filing jointly, but your parents are on the house along

with the two of you, then divide the value by four. If you estimate the value of the home at $100,000, then the value you would list is $50,000 ($100,000 ÷ 4 – the two of you and your two parents) x 2 (both of you filing jointly). Using the same situation, if you file without your spouse, you list a value of $25,000 ($100,000 ÷ 4 – you, your spouse, and your two parents.)

55.   In the fifth column, note the liens on the property. These may include:

♦ Mortgages
♦ Home equity loans
♦ Property taxes
♦ Tax liens
♦ Judgment liens

56.   Add all liens specific to the property and list the total in the fifth column.

57.   If you have another piece of real estate, go back to item 50 and repeat the process. You'll go through this process for every piece of real estate you own. If you run out of space on the page, add additional sheets. When you've listed all the real estate you own, go to the next step.

58.   Add all the values listed in the fourth column. Put that number in the box at the bottom of the column next to Total.

59.   We're done, now we'll go back to

http://www.uscourts.gov/bkforms/bankruptcy_forms.html.

There you will open B6B – Schedule B – Personal Property.

60.   On the top left of the page, next to "In re" write your name and, if this is a joint petition, add your spouse's name.

61.   Personal property is how attorneys describe everything you own besides real estate, and you're required to list these things on Schedule B. Don't worry. Just because property is listed here doesn't mean you'll lose it during this process. I'll discuss how you keep property in Chapter 10 of this book. For now, carefully list everything so you won't be accused of fraud because you didn't list all your assets.

62.   Most of the items listed on this schedule are self-explanatory. We will only hit the highlights.

63.   If you run out of space, you can add additional pages.

64.   Item 1 – cash on hand – is basically money you have around the house. For column 3 (description), write "cash on hand," designate who the money belongs to (h for husband, w for wife, j for joint if it belongs to both of you) in Column 3. In the last column write the value of the money on hand.

65. Item 2 – bank accounts – list all bank accounts, checking accounts, savings accounts, credit union accounts, certificates of deposit, etc. as follows:

2. Checking, savings or other financial accounts, certificates of deposit or shares in banks, savings and loan, thrift, building and loan, and homestead associations or credit unions, brokerage houses, or cooperatives.	checking and savings accounts Location: Bank of America	J	$500

66. The value of the bank account should be your current balance in that account. If you're using funds from one of these bank accounts for filing fees, you can reduce that account by the $299 fee. Again, designate who the account belongs to in Column 4. Do this for each bank account your name is on, even if the bank account has no money in it.

67. Item 3 – Security Deposits – This includes security deposits with your landlord or for your utilities. Some utilities require you to put a deposit down before they provide you with service, and that's the kind of security deposit we're talking about here. Complete this line as you did line 2.

68. Item 4 – Household Goods and Furnishings – Here we're getting to the meat of the matter. For all the assets you're listing in Schedule B, you need liquidation value – the amount you'd get if you sold the items in a garage sale or on eBay. Don't list the amount of money you paid for the items, the amount it would take to replace the property, or the amount of money the property is insured for. Use the lowest possible valuation. Realistic, but low. For this line, imagine you're moving everything out of your home onto the front lawn and holding a garage sale. How much money will you make? That's the number you put down here.

69. Items 5 through 8 are self-explanatory. If you own the property described here, list that property and the liquidation value for that property.

70. Item 9 – Interests in Insurance Policies – the key they are looking for here is life insurance, in particular cash value or whole life insurance. This is the kind of life insurance you can borrow from, and if you stop making monthly payments on it, you will continue to be covered. This kind of insurance is different from term life insurance. Term life insurance simply pays money to your beneficiaries if you die. It has no on-going value and will immediately terminate coverage if you stop making payments. If you aren't sure what kind

of insurance you have, ask your insurance agent. I suggest you list all life insurance you have, whether term, cash-value, whole life, or through your employer. Term policies should be valued at one dollar. Most policies offered as a benefit by employers are term policies. For cash value policies, look at a statement from your insurance company to determine the surrender value. That number is probably much lower than the amount your beneficiaries will receive upon your death. The surrender value is what you put in the fifth column.

71.   Item 10 – Annuities – If you have an annuity, you'll know it. Annuities are like reverse life insurance policies. You give a certain amount of money to a life insurance company, and when you reach the specified age, the company begins paying you a certain amount of money per year, or per month. The value for this property is the total value of the annuity, not just the monthly payment. That amount should be listed on a statement you receive.

72.   Item 11 – Education IRA or 529 Plan – note this interest would be for a plan you own.

73.   Go to the next page.

74.   On the top left of the page, next to "In re" write your name and add your spouse's name if this is a joint petition.

75.   Item 12 – This is where you list your 401Ks, IRAs, and any other retirement savings plans you own. Don't worry, these retirement savings are usually fully protected through this process.

76.   Item 13 – Business Ownership Interests – You should list two types of assets here. First, list any stock you own that isn't part of a 401k, IRA, or other retirement savings plan you listed in item 12. This stock could be in a mutual fund. Determine the current value of the stock by looking up a stock quote or a statement from your broker. Place this value in column 5. The other kind of asset you list here is ownership interest in a small business. A key here is determining two things: first, your share of the business (you may only own a certain percentage of the business if you own it with someone else), and the value of the business. For most businesses, I suggest you value the business by listing all assets that actually belong to the business itself. Remember, these are not assets that belong to you – they belong to the business. For example, people sometimes own a vehicle used for a business, but the business doesn't legally own that vehicle. The same may be true for equipment and other property. List all the assets for the business. Assets may include bank accounts, accounts receivable (funds owed by customers to the business), equipment, etc. Then list the debts for the business. The result should look something like this:

13 Stock and interest in incorporated and unincorporated businesses. Itemize.	My business Inc. - only assets are bank account (Chase Bank, $1000), accounts receivable ($500), and equipment ($500). Liabilities include debts owed to suppliers ($500) and business credit card ($500) Location: My home address, Anytown USA	H	$1,000

77.   Item 14 – Interests in Partnerships or Joint Ventures – complete this item the same way as Item 13. This item specifically refers to "partnerships" where you might have a partner, as opposed to a corporation where you would own a percentage of the business with someone else.

78.   Item 15 – list savings bonds, corporate bonds, or municipal bonds you own. If your children have bonds their grandparents and other relatives gave them, do not list those here. They will go elsewhere.

79.   Item 16 – does anyone owe you money for any reason (except for child support and alimony, we'll get to that later)? If yes, list it here.

80.   Item 17 – Here's where you will list alimony or child support owed to you. List it whether you think you will get the money or not.

81.   Item 18 – Here's a tricky one. Look at your last tax return. Add your refunds from the state, federal, and (if applicable) municipal governments. Then, based upon the month, divide the total refunds by 12. Multiply the resulting number by the number of months that have passed and put that number there. For example, if you file in June and received tax refunds of $1200 last year, you will list "anticipated tax refund" for the description, and value that tax refund at $600 (since June is the sixth month, you divide $1200 by 12 and multiply that by 6 to get $600). Essentially, you've already earned your tax refund for next year for the months that have already passed. One more issue. Say you are filing for Bankruptcy in February and you haven't yet filed your tax return for this year. You are owed your tax refund for last year, plus the amount of the tax refund you have already earned for this year. So, using the same example from above, your anticipated tax refund would be $1400 (that is $1200 for the year before, and $200 because February is the second month, you divide $1200 by 12 and multiply that number by 2 to get $200).

82.   Item 19 is where you list real estate interests not listed on Schedule A for some reason. If you have these types of real estate interests, you should speak with an attorney.

83.   Item 20 – Has someone close to you recently passed away? If so, did that person leave you property, money, or life insurance? This item is relevant if you expect to inherit something, but haven't yet

received the inheritance.

84. Item 21 – list if you are suing someone or thinking of suing someone for any reason.

85. Go to the next page.

86. On the top left of the page, next to "In re" write your name. Add your spouse's name if this is a joint petition.

87. Items 22 to 24 are self-explanatory. You should know if you own these types of intellectual property.

88. This is where you list your vehicles. Cars, trucks, trailers, motorcycles, four-wheelers, campers, and snowmobiles all go here. Note this only includes vehicles you own, whether you owe money on them or not. Leasing a vehicle is not an ownership interest – it's like renting. The only exception to that rule is if you pre-paid a car lease up front. In that case, the lease itself may have value and should be listed here. You need to address two key issues here: who the vehicle belongs to, and valuation. All that matters here is whose name is on the title. Take the time to look at the titles to your vehicles and make sure you list the correct owner of each vehicle. To value the vehicle, go to one of the following two websites:

www.kbb.com or www.nadaguides.com.

Between those two websites, you should be able to get a price for almost any vehicle. Make sure you list the vehicle's year and mileage in the description. Remember, you want to use the low value for the vehicle, because we're talking about liquidation value. When you're finished the entry should look like this:

25. Automobiles, trucks, trailers, and other vehicles and accessories	2005 Chevrolet Impala, 60,000 miles Location: My home address, Anytown USA	J	$3,950

89. Item 26 – Here you list boats and any other kind of watercraft. For valuation purposes, I recommend using

www.nadaguides.com.

90. Item 27 – If you can afford to own aircraft, you can afford to pay an attorney. Enough said.

91. Item 28 is where you would list office equipment, furnishings and supplies. Remember, computers and computer equipment decline in value quickly. Don't list what you paid for the equipment here or what it would cost to replace it. List what you could sell it for. Unless the equipment is basically brand new, its value is minimal.

92.   Item 29 – The classic case here is a mechanic who owns his own tools, but keeps them at the job site. Mechanics often own tools they keep at work, and this is where you list such property. Again, use the value you could sell the property for, not how much you'd pay to replace it.

93.   Item 30 – Inventory - this is most often used in business filings. If you have this kind of property, you'll know.

94.   Item 31 – No matter how valuable your dog or cat is to you, unless it's a prize-winning purebred you show and use for breeding, it has no value to your creditors. Put zero for the value here.

95.   Items 32 to 34 are self-explanatory.

96.   Item 35 is the last one. Here you list any property not mentioned elsewhere.

97.   You can add additional pages if needed. If you do add pages, you must put how many pages you added in the space at the bottom of the page that says "___ continuation sheets attached."

98.   Add all the numbers you've listed in the fifth column on all the pages of Schedule B and put that number in the box for the total at the bottom right. Make sure this number includes all the values listed on the continuation sheets.

99.   Congratulations, you are finished with Schedule B. Now let's move on to Schedule D. Don't worry, we'll get back to Schedule C in Chapter 10 of this book. For now, go back to the website

http://www.uscourts.gov/bkforms/bankruptcy_forms.html.

There you will open B6D – "Schedule D - Creditors Holding Secured Claims."

100.   On the top left of the page, next to "In re" write your name. If this is a joint petition, add your spouse's name.

102.   Secured claims include the following:
   ♦   Mortgages
   ♦   Home equity loans
   ♦   Property taxes
   ♦   Car loans
   ♦   Boat loans
   ♦   Tax liens
   ♦   Judgment liens
   ♦   Any kind of loan that has a security interest or a lien on property that belongs to you

103.   If you do not have any of the kind of debts listed in paragraph 102, then check the box under the text and go to item 111. If you do have some of these debts, go to the next paragraph.

104. Note that you can add continuation sheets if you run out of space.

105. List each debt you have from paragraph 102 on a separate line on Schedule D. This is how you will complete each line:

   ◆ At the top of the box in the first column, write the last four digits of the account number for that creditor. If you don't know the account number, use the last four digits of your Social Security number.

   ◆ Under the account number space in the first column, write the name, mailing address, city, state, and zip code for the creditor.

   ◆ Put an X in the second column if someone not filing with you is a co-signer on this debt.

   ◆ Who is liable for this debt? In a joint filing, you need to designate if the husband is liable (H), the wife (W), or both of you (J). Put the correct letter in column three.

   ◆ When did you take out this loan? List the year at the top of the box in column four. Leave plenty of space, because we need to write several things in that box.

   ◆ What kind of loan is it? Is it a first mortgage, second mortgage, home equity loan, tax lien, judgment lien, car loan, boat loan, or a loan you secured with your vehicle or boat (that would be called a non-pmsi)? List the type of loan just below the year in column four.

   ◆ What property is the loan secured by? Is it your home, vacation property, vacant property, investment property, a vehicle (if you have more than one, write the kind of vehicle), or a boat? Below the kind of loan, write the property it is attached to in column four.

   ◆ Lastly, where it says "value" at the bottom of the box in column four, list the value of the property secured by the loan. Look at where you have this property listed on Schedule A or Schedule B to see what value you gave that property, and put that value next to the "value $" at the bottom of the box in column four.

   ◆ Next, if you believe you don't actually owe this money, put an X in column 7 under "disputed."

   ◆ How much do you owe on this loan? Put that amount in column eight.

   ◆ Subtract the number in column eight from the number next to "value $" in column four. If that number is more than zero, put the resulting number in column nine. If that number is less than zero, simply put zero in column nine.

   ◆ The result should look something like this:

Account No. 1234							
CitiMortgage PO Box 79022 St. Louis, MO 63179	X	J	2005 First Mortgage Home VALUE $100,000			$110,000	$10,000

106.   Repeat this process for each secured debt you have.

107.   The second page for this schedule at the website is the continuation page. If you need to add more than one continuation page, keep using that second page. Once you've entered all your secured creditors, count how many continuation pages you have and write that number in the space at the bottom left of the first page of Schedule D. Then, at the bottom left of each continuation page, number them "Sheet no. 1 of 3 continuation sheets."

108.   Add the numbers in column eight for each page in this schedule. Put that number in the box that is second from the bottom of column eight for each page in the schedule.

109.   Add the numbers in column nine for each page in this schedule. Put that number in the box that is second from the bottom of column nine for each page in the schedule.

110.   On the last page of Schedule D, add the totals of all pages for columns eight and nine. Put the totals for all pages in the bottom boxes of columns eight and nine on the last page of this schedule.

111.   Congratulations, you've completed Schedule D. Go back to the website

http://www.uscourts.gov/bkforms/bankruptcy_forms.html.

There you will open B6E – "Schedule E - Creditors Holding Unsecured Priority Claims."

112.   On the top left of the page, next to "In re" write your name. If this is a joint petition, add your spouse's name.

113.   Priority claims include the following:
   ♦ Taxes owed
   ♦ Child support owed
   ♦ Alimony owed
   ♦ Debts you owe as a result of an accident while you were intoxicated

114.   If you do not have any of the kind of debts listed in paragraph 113, then check the first box and go to paragraph 127. If you do have some of these debts, move to the next paragraph.

115.   Note that you can add continuation sheets if you run out of space.

116.   First you need to check what kinds of debts you have.

- ◆ If you owe child support or alimony, check the second box on the first page of Schedule E for "Domestic Support Obligations." You should be prepared for the fact that as you go through this process, the person to whom you owe child support will be made aware of your Bankruptcy even if you're not behind in your payments. As a result, you may want to give that person a heads-up.
- ◆ If you owe taxes, check the third box on the second page of Schedule E where it says "Taxes and Certain Other Debts Owed to Governmental Units."
- ◆ If you owe debts resulting from an accident that occurred while you were intoxicated, check the last box on page two of Schedule E where it says "Claims for Death of Personal Injury While Debtor Was Intoxicated."

117. On the top left of the second page of Schedule E, next to "In re" write your name. If this is a joint petition, add your spouse's name.

118. For each kind of debt you checked from paragraph 116, you need to do a separate continuation page. As a result, if you checked one kind of debt from paragraph 116, you need one continuation page. If you checked all three, you need three continuation pages. At the bottom of page two of Schedule E, write how many continuation pages you will be adding.

119. Go to the first continuation page for Schedule E. On the top left of the second page of Schedule E, next to "In re" write your name and, if this is a joint petition, your spouse's name.

120. Immediately below the headline it says "Schedule E – Creditors Holding Unsecured Priority Claims (Continuation Sheet)" and to the right, above the table "Type of Priority for Claims Listed on This Sheet." To the left of that statement, write the kind of debts you'll be listing on this page. Remember, you can only have one kind of priority debt on each continuation page. So to the left of that statement, write one of the following for this page:
- ◆ Domestic Support Obligations.
- ◆ Taxes and Certain Other Debts Owed to Governmental Units.
- ◆ Claims for Death of Personal Injury While Debtor Was Intoxicated.

121. For each debt of the kind you're listing on this page, you need to fill out a separate line as follows:
- ◆ In column one at the top of each box, place the last four digits of your account number. If you don't have an account number, use the last four digits of your Social Security number.
- ◆ Below the account number in the first column, write the name, mailing address, city, state and zip code for the creditor.

♦ If you have a co-debtor (i.e. for taxes if your spouse isn't filing jointly with you), put an X in column two.

♦ If you are filing jointly, state who owes the debt in column three: h for husband, w for wife, or j for both.

♦ In the fourth column, write at the top of the box the year you started owing that debt. For taxes, it may be for number of years. If so, list them. List all taxes you owe, whether city, state or federal. You only need to go back three years, however. Any taxes four or more years old are not entitled to priority, and, as a result, those older taxes will not get listed here. Stay near the top of the box, because you still have things to add.

♦ Below the year in the fourth column, write what kind of debt it is – i.e. income taxes, sales taxes, child support, or alimony.

♦ If you dispute that you owe this debt, put an X in column seven.

♦ In column eight, write how much the creditor claims you owe.

♦ Typically, for these kinds of debt, the entire amount is entitled to priority. Put the full amount you owe this creditor in column nine. Put a zero in column ten.

♦ A completed entry should look like this:

Account No. 1234								
Internal Revenue Service PO Box 21126 Philadelphia, PA 19114		J	2007 Income taxes			X	$2000	$2000	$0

122. Go through the steps in paragraph 121 for each creditor.

123. When you finish this page, total columns eight, nine, and ten and write the totals in the three boxes at the bottom of the columns.

124. At the bottom left of the page, write that this sheet is sheet 1 of however many continuation pages you need to use.

125. For each type of priority debt, return to item 120 to start a new page. If you finish a page for all the kinds of debt you have, go to the next item.

126. Go through all the continuation sheets for Schedule E. Add the subtotals at the bottom of columns eight, nine, and ten.

♦ On the last of the continuation sheets, place the total of all the column eight subtotals in the white box, one line up from the bottom of column eight.

♦ On the last of the continuation sheets, put the total of all the column nine subtotals in the white box at the bottom of column nine.

- On the last of the continuation sheets, write the total of all the column ten subtotals in the white box at the bottom of column ten.

127. Now you're done with Schedule E. Next, go back to the website

    http://www.uscourts.gov/bkforms/bankruptcy_forms.html.

    There you will open up for B6F – "Schedule F - Creditors Holding Unsecured Nonpriority Claims."

128. On the top left of the page, next to "In re" write your name. If this is a joint petition, add your spouse's name.

129. This is the schedule where you list all other creditors. Note that you need to list all your creditors. With few exceptions, you won't get to keep any credit cards you owe money on. You can't keep any debts you have out of the process. The type of debts you list here include:

    - Credit cards
    - Medical bills
    - Veterinary bills
    - Taxes that are four or more years old (as long as the taxing entity has not filed a tax lien against you – if they have, you'll know)
    - Service bills, such as gym membership, lawn-cutting, home repairs, and child care bills
    - Personal loans
    - Past due utility bills
    - Gambling debts

130. The first page is the first page of this schedule. The second page is the continuation sheet. You can copy the continuation sheet as many times as you need in order to list all your creditors.

131. For each creditor, fill out a separate line as follows:

    - In column one at the top of each box, put the last four digits of your account number. If you don't have an account number, use the last four digits of your Social Security number.
    - Below the account number in the first column, write the name, mailing address, city, state, and zip code for the creditor.
    - If you have a co-debtor (i.e. for a joint credit card if your spouse is not filing jointly with you), put an X in column two.
    - If you are filing jointly, in column three state who owes the debt: h for husband, w for wife, or j for both.
    - In the fourth column, write at the top of the box the year you started owing that debt. For credit cards, list when you last used the card. Stay near the top of the box, because you have more writing to do.

- ◆ Right below the year in the fourth column, write what kind of debt this is – i.e. credit card debt, consumer debt, personal loan, trade debt (business debt).
- ◆ If you dispute you owe this debt, put an X in column seven.
- ◆ In column eight, write how much the creditor claims you owe.
- ◆ A completed entry should look like this:

ACCOUNT NO. 1234 Chase Bank Po Box 100018 Kennesaw, GA 30156		J	2010 Credit card debt			X	$2000

132. Go through the steps in paragraph 131 for each creditor. Make sure every creditor you owe money to is listed, because this is how you're protected from them. In certain cases, if you don't list a creditor they can still come after you once your case is over.

133. As you complete the first page of Schedule F, add the amounts listed in column eight and put the total in the box for "Subtotal" at the bottom of that column.

134. If you're finished, put the "subtotal" figure in the "total" box at the bottom of column eight. If you still have creditors to enter, leave that box blank.

135. If you need to add more creditors once the first page is full, go to the second page of Schedule F. That is the continuation sheet, and you can make as many copies of this page as you need. Continue to add creditors as described in paragraph 131.

136. As you complete a continuation page for Schedule F, total the amounts in column eight and put that figure in the "Subtotal" box at the bottom of that column. If you need more sheets, use copies of the second page.

137. Continue as described in paragraphs 134 to 135 until you've listed all your creditors.

140. Once you've listed the creditors, count how many continuation sheets (not including the first page of Schedule F) you used. On the first page of Schedule F, on the bottom left of the page, write the number of continuation sheets. If you were able to fit all the creditors on the first page, put a zero in that space.

141. On the bottom left of all continuation sheets, number the continuation sheets as follows: "Sheet no ____ of ____ continuation sheets attached."

142. Add the subtotals at the bottom of the first page of Schedule F and all continuation sheets. On the last page of the continuation sheets for Schedule F, in the box for "Total" at the bottom of column eight, write the sum of all subtotals.

143. Good job. Now you've finished Schedule F. Next, go back to the website

    http://www.uscourts.gov/bkforms/bankruptcy_forms.html.

    There you will open up for B6G – Schedule G – Executory Contracts and Unexpired Leases.

144. On the top left of the page, next to "In re" write your name. If this is a joint petition, add your spouse's name.

145. An executory contract is a contract where both you and the other party have on-going obligations. Key examples of executory contracts and leases include:
    ♦ A lease of your apartment or home
    ♦ A lease for lot rent for your trailer park
    ♦ A car lease – remember we said car leases would not be listed in Schedule B
    ♦ A cell phone contract
    ♦ A contract for use of a storage unit
    ♦ Gym memberships
    ♦ Lawn care contracts
    ♦ A timeshare contract

146. If you have no executory contracts or leases as described in 145, simply check the box right under the text and move on to 150. Note that month-to-month leases are not on-going contracts or leases, since your obligation ends at the end of each month.

147. If you have executory contracts or leases as described in 145, complete this schedule by listing each contract or lease as follows:
    ♦ In the left column, list the name, mailing address, city, state, and zip of the other parties to the lease or contract (i.e. your landlord).
    ♦ In the right column, describe the contract – i.e. lease of residential real estate, lease of vehicle, cell phone contract, etc.

148. Complete the steps in 147 for each contract or lease that is on-going.

149. If you need to add additional sheets, make copies of the Schedule G sheet.

150. After listing all your on-going leases or contracts, you can move on to the next schedule. Go back to the website

    http://www.uscourts.gov/bkforms/bankruptcy_forms.html.

    There you will open up for B6H –Schedule H - Co-debtors.

151. On the top left of the page, next to "In re" write your name. If this is a joint petition, add your spouse's name.

152. Co-debtors are co-signers on your debts. Even if you're listed first on the debt, the co-debtor is equally liable for that debt. As a result, they need to be notified of your Bankruptcy, since the filing will directly affect them. Examples of co-debtors include your spouse if you aren't filing jointly, or a parent or friend who co-signed a debt for you.

153. If you have no co-debtors, check the box under the text. You're finished with this schedule.

154. If you do have co-debtors, write the name and mailing address of each person in the column on the left, and the name and address of the creditors for which that person is a co-debtor on the right. Repeat this process on a separate line for each co-debtor. If needed, you can copy this page and use it as a continuation sheet.

155. After listing all your co-debtors, you can move on to the next schedule. At the website

    http://www.uscourts.gov/bkforms/bankruptcy_forms.html,

    you will open B6I – Schedule I - Current Income of Individual Debtor(s).

156. On the top left of the page, next to "In re" write your name. If this is a joint petition, add your spouse's name.

157. You have to show the court you cannot afford to pay back your creditors. To do so, you create a budget for your expenses. I suggest you take your time on Schedule I and the next schedule, Schedule J. Not surprisingly, Schedule J deals with your expenses.

158. To complete this form, follow these directions:
    ♦ On the top left of the table, place your marital status. Here you type "single," "married," "divorced," "widowed," or "separated."
    ♦ On the second line of the table next to RELATIONSHIP(S), note your relationship to all your dependents. Remember, for Bankruptcy purposes, dependants may include people other than those who are dependents for tax purposes. For example, an elderly relative who lives with you, a grown child who's unemployed, or a boyfriend/girlfriend who is unemployed, could all be considered your dependents. Don't put names in this box, just relationships, such as: son, daughter, grandson, grand-daughter, step-son, step-daughter, father, mother, etc. You get the picture.
    ♦ To the right of where you list the relationships, place the dependents' ages in the order you listed the dependents.
    ♦ Below that, under "Debtor," list your occupation (what you do for a living), your employer, how long you've been employed there, and the address of your employer. If you're unemployed,

write "unemployed." If you're retired, write "retired." If you're disabled, write "disabled." If you're a homemaker, write "homemaker." You get the picture. If you have multiple jobs, list your main employer here. If you're self-employed, write "self-employed" for your employer.

♦ If you're married, unless you're filing an affidavit of separate households as we described in Chapter 5, you need to list your spouse's employment status and income even if you aren't filing jointly. Follow the same directions as above, then move to the next step.

♦ Now we start with your income. Under the column for Debtor underneath the table, fill in the lines. First, list your monthly gross income. Typically, this income will match the monthly gross income you calculated from your paystubs for the Means Test in Chapter 5. If your pay has changed, you've lost overtime, or you're no longer employed by the employer listed in the Means Test, put your current income going forward. Don't stick with the amount listed in the Means Test if it's no longer accurate. Remember, here we're listing the income for your main job where the employer is listed on the top. Furthermore, remember the first line is your gross, pretax income.

♦ I usually include overtime on line 1, since that gross income is an average of all your income over the last six months unless your income has changed. As a result, I typically skip line 2, and this has never been an issue.

♦ On line 3, put the amount from line 1.

♦ Next, go back to the calculations you made from your pay stubs for the Means Test. On line **4a**, list your tax deductions from this job. On line **4b**, list insurance deductions. On line **4c**, list your union dues. Remember, the figures you put here should be per month. On line **4d**, list any other deductions, such as 401K loans, charitable contributions, health savings accounts, or mandatory retirement deductions. If the retirement deductions are not mandatory, don't list them.

♦ For item 5, add all the deductions listed in items **4a** through **4d**.

♦ Next, subtract line 5 from line 3. Put that number in line 6.

♦ Use line 7 if you are self-employed. If so, list the average monthly gross income you receive from self-employment. Again, I suggest you base this number on the calculations you made for the Means Test in Chapter 5.

♦ Use line 8 to record any rental income you receive. You will deduct the expenses for this income on Schedule J.

- Use line 9 if you receive interest and dividends. Put that average monthly figure here.
- Line 10 is where you list alimony or child support you receive.
- In line 11, list Social Security, Unemployment Compensation, Food Stamps, or other government income you receive.
- If you receive a monthly pension, put that amount in 12. If you have more than one pension, add them and put that number in line 12.
- In line 13, list any other monthly income you receive. This includes second jobs. For a second job only list your net, after taxes, take home income in line 13.
- Add lines 7 though 13. Put that total in line 14.
- Add lines 14 and 6. Put that number in line 15.
- Next, if you're married, whether filing jointly or individually, you must list your spouse's income unless you're separated and are filing the declaration of separate households described in Chapter 5 of this book. To do so, complete the lines under Spouse the same way.
- Once you've recorded all the income coming into the household, add the two lines in column 15 and put that total in line 16.
- If you anticipate any Increases or decreases in income over the next year, describe what you expect in line 17.

159. You've now finished Schedule I. Let's move on to Schedule J. Return to the website

    http://www.uscourts.gov/bkforms/bankruptcy_forms.html,

    where you will open up B6J – "Schedule J- Current Expenditures of Individual Debtor(s)."

160. This is the next part of the budget equation: your expenses. The court wants to know you cannot afford to pay back your creditors. Do not include payments on any credit cards or other debts in this schedule. The only debts you include here are mortgage payments and car payments. If you have a payment arrangement to repay taxes, you might want to include that monthly figure as well. The same for student loan payments. Other than that, do not include any debt payments.

161. Also, do not double-count expenses you already listed on Schedule I. If you pay health insurance through your paycheck, don't list the cost of health insurance on Schedule J even though there is a place for it. You only get to show a cost once.

162. This is the schedule where you detail how you spend your money

every month. You must think seriously about how you actually use your income. Most people tend to understate their expenses. As a result, the first time you go through this process it will probably seem you have lots of money left over. Think honestly about your expenses.

- ♦ Line 1 is for your rent or mortgage payments. If you have more than one mortgage on your home, add up the monthly payments. If you pay a mortgage on a manufactured home and lot rent, total those monthly bills for this line.
- ♦ Do you have an escrow account on your mortgage through which you pay property taxes? And what about your homeowners' insurance? Just below line 1, check *yes* for a and/or b if you do make these payments through your mortgage escrow. If not, check *no*. If you rent, and you do not separately pay these expenses, also check *yes*.
- ♦ Line 2 includes utilities.
  - a is where you list the average monthly cost for electric service and heating
  - b is where you list your water and sewer bill (if you pay for it separately)
  - c is where you list telephone bills, including cell phone bills. If you have both a cell phone and a land line, add those monthly bills together for this line.
  - d is where you list other utilities, such as homeowner's association fees, cable services, Internet service, trash pick-up, or other similar monthly bills you pay.
- ♦ Home maintenance – put something here! You certainly spend at least $50 to $100 per month on maintenance, no matter where you live. If you've had extraordinary expenses such as a roof, furnace, or window replacement, take that expense, divide it by 12, and add that number to your monthly maintenance figure. If you have a high number, be prepared to show receipts. But if the bill is legitimate, you won't have a problem adding it into this calculation.
- ♦ Line 4 is where you list your average grocery bill, and I guarantee you'll initially underestimate this amount. Consider everything you spend for groceries on an on-going basis. Also, if you or your children have to purchase lunch at work or school, add that monthly expense as well.
- ♦ Clothing – again, put a number here. Even the worst-dressed person should have $100 listed. Unless you have to purchase certain clothing for work, don't go much over $150. Anything above that will raise questions.

- Laundry/Dry Cleaning – what do you spend on laundry supplies, the laundromat, and dry cleaning? Add those figures and put the number here.
- Medical/Dental expenses – What do you spend out-of-pocket on medical expenses? Don't include the cost of health insurance here. This is how much you spend on average for prescriptions, co-pays, vitamins, glasses, braces, dentists, and all other medical needs. If you get prescriptions every three months, take that cost and divide it by three. Don't leave this number blank. Even if you're healthy, you need a number here in case you get sick.
- Transportation – This is not where you put your car payments or car insurance. Instead, list your monthly costs for gas, maintenance, oil changes, and public transportation.
- Recreation – I like to keep this line to a minimum. It's hard to justify a lavish recreation budget when your creditors are getting the shaft. Try to keep this line below $50.
- Charitable contributions – It's acceptable, and even encouraged for you to make charitable contributions despite your bankruptcy. What you cannot do is suddenly start making charitable contributions right before you file Bankruptcy. However, if you routinely make certain charitable contributions, including tithing to a church, you may continue doing so, and you can list that monthly expense on this line.
- Insurance – list insurance expenses you directly pay. Do not double-count insurance you deducted elsewhere. For example, if you pay your health insurance and life insurance through work and you listed those deductions on Schedule I, do not separately list those expenses again here. Also, if you pay your homeowners' insurance through your mortgage payment, do not separately list that expense here.
- Taxes – If you're self-employed and separately withhold your own taxes, list the average monthly expense you pay. If you pay real estate taxes outside of your mortgage (of if you don't have a mortgage on your home), take the annual amount of property taxes you pay, divide that by 12, and list the monthly average on this line.
- Installment payments – Here you list all your installment payments such as car payments, boat payments, appliance payments, etc. Only list payments you want to keep making because you intend to keep the collateral. If you have a boat payment and you can no longer afford to keep that boat, don't list the boat payment as an expense on this schedule.

- ♦ Alimony, maintenance, and support paid to others – This is where you list child support. However, if your child support comes directly out of your paycheck and you already listed that deduction in schedule I, do not double-count that expense. If you help support an elderly relative, list the amount of money you spend to help that person.
- ♦ I've always felt line 15 is a repeat of line 14. Leave it blank unless you can come up with a reason to list a specific expense.
- ♦ Business expenses – if you own your own business, this is where you note your expenses. Be prepared to attach a detailed list explaining these expenses.
- ♦ Other – Remember to keep these expenses reasonable. Here are some examples of other expenses you may want to list:
  - Haircuts
  - Cigarettes
  - Veterinary care and pet food
  - Childcare
  - Bank fees
  - Other personal expenses.

163. After you've spent some time on this exercise, add lines 1 through 17 and put that number in line 18 (with the box around it).

164. In 20a, place the income listed in line 16 on Schedule I. In 20b put the number from line 18 on this schedule (the one with the box around it). Then subtract 20b from 20a. How much money do you have left over at the end of the month? If you have more than $100 left at the end of each month, you probably cannot file Chapter 7, since you can afford to pay your creditors. If the figures you come up with don't mesh with reality, then you need to revisit your expenses. You've probably understated them, which is typical. Keep working with those numbers until the number in 20c looks like the amount of money you actually have at the end of every month after you pay your bills.

Congratulations. You've completed a major step in your Bankruptcy petition. We still have specialized schedules to revisit, but you're well on your way to being finished. Let's move on to the process you use to keep your property and assets.

Chapter 10

Can I Keep My Stuff In Bankruptcy?
Schedule C and the Statement of Intention

*P*eople often come to my office with visions of creditors marching into their homes and hauling off their furniture, clothing, and computers. This almost never happens. In this chapter we'll look at the procedure that allows you to protect your assets.

You do have some basis for concern. The theory of Chapter 7 Bankruptcy is that you give up not only your debts, but also your assets. In theory, you get a complete fresh start, a blank sheet of paper. With business, when you file Chapter 7 Bankruptcy, the business is over. You shut the doors, liquidate everything, and walk away. Creditors each get their share of the scraps.

Congress understood, however, that this kind of clean sweep doesn't work for people. You need a home, a car, clothing, tools you use for work, retirement savings, and many other things. Much of your property is worth a lot more to you than to your creditors, such as your wedding ring, family pictures, and heirloom furniture. As a result, Congress has included exemptions in the Bankruptcy Code – a list of certain types of assets you can keep. Congress says you can keep your 401K. With other assets, Congress placed a limit on the value of items they let you keep. You can retain the tools you use for work, but only $2000 worth. You can hold onto a cash value or whole life insurance policy, but only if it has a surrender value of $10,775 or less. In fact, for most assets, Congress placed a limit on the total value you can keep. Exceptions include the 401K or IRA.

This policy actually makes sense when you think about it. How would it be fair for somebody who owns a huge, beautiful house free and clear, to walk away from his or her debts scott free? How would it be fair for someone with thousands of dollars worth of jewelry to keep all the jewelry and not pay her creditors? Even Congress sometimes makes sense.

Congress has given you one more advantage as you consider exemption – a wildcard exemption you can use for anything you own: cash, stocks, bonds, collections, money in bank accounts, jewelry, extra vehicles, whatever. But this exemption has a twist. You automatically get $1075 worth of exemption to use as a wildcard. Furthermore, if you haven't used all your exemption for your home, you can use up to $10,125 of the homestead exemption for anything else. As a result, if you rent, or if your mortgages eat up most of the equity in your home, you can use up to $11,200 as an exemption for anything you have. This is a powerful tool.

That brings us to the next point. You don't need to protect equity in any property that is eaten up by secured debts like mortgages, car loans, boat loans, home equity loans, judgment liens, tax liens, property taxes, etc. from your creditors. You only need to protect the equity you own in the property from the creditors. Therefore, especially in this real estate market, the value of the homestead exemption is actually quite substantial. Let me demonstrate.

Let's say your home is worth $100,000. If you have a first mortgage of $80,000 on the property, a home equity loan of $15,000, and you owe $3000 in property taxes, then you actually only have $2000 in equity in the home ($100,000 - $80,000 - $15,000 - $3000 = $2000). Obviously, with $20,200 in exemption available to protect your home, there's plenty of exemption available and you can use the full $11,200 as a wildcard exemption.

Also bear in mind that you only need to exempt your share of the equity. Say, for example, you're married but filing individually, and your spouse co-owns your home with you. If that's the case, then you only own half the equity in your home. As a result, in the example above, you would only need to exempt $1000 of equity, since the other $1000 is owned by your spouse. In addition to your husband or wife, if your mother is also on the deed, then you only own 1/3 of the equity, and so on. This rule applies to any kind of property. Say you and your mother are both on the title to your car. In that case, you only own half of the car and only need to protect half the value of it.

There's more. If you file jointly, you essentially double your exemptions. So if you're filing jointly, any assets you own together can be half exempt by you and half exempt by your spouse. Say you have $40,000 of equity in your home. You can't protect that equity by yourself, but if you own the home jointly with your spouse, you can exempt $20,000 worth of equity and your spouse can exempt $20,000 worth. And you'd still have $400 between the two of you left for the wildcard exemption.

I have one word of caution regarding jointly exempting property. In most states, spouses can own property separate from one another. Just because you're married doesn't mean you and your spouse jointly own everything. However, Arizona, California, Idaho, Louisiana, Nevada, New Mexico, Texas, Washington, and Wisconsin are community property states. Anything one spouse acquires in the marriage automatically becomes community property, essentially jointly owned by both spouses. In any other state, you go by what the paperwork says: the deed to real estate, the title to the car or boat, the name on the bank account or financial investments, etc. In most states, you need to check your paperwork to make sure property is jointly owned before both spouses can use an exemption to protect it.

Even if both of you own the property, you don't need to use both spouse's exemption. Suppose you and your spouse each have a car and both your names are on both cars. Each of you can only exempt one car. As a result, one spouse can use his or her vehicle exemption for one car, while the other spouse can use his or her vehicle exemption for the other car. In that way, both vehicles will be protected.

Sounds great, doesn't it? But Congress threw in a wrench. You knew this was coming, didn't you? Before Congress included the exemptions in the Bankruptcy Code, every state had already adopted its own exemptions. Generally speaking, the exemptions from one state to the other are similar, but there are striking exceptions. Florida and Texas, for example, are the only states where you can exempt your home no matter how much it's worth. That's how O.J. Simpson managed to live in Florida despite having a multi-million dollar wrongful death judgment against him. His pension and 401K were fully exempt, and so was his house. In any state other than Texas or Florida, the people with judgments against him could collect against his home. But not there. In Florida, all his assets are fully exempt.

So the states had their own exemptions, and they didn't want Congress raining on their parade. As is typical for politicians, they came up with a compromise. If you live in one of these states - Alaska, Arkansas, Connecticut, District of Columbia, Hawaii, Kentucky, Massachusetts, Michigan, Minnesota, New Hampshire, New Mexico, New Jersey, Pennsylvania, Puerto Rico, Rhode Island, Texas, Vermont, Washington, Wisconsin – then you can choose which set of exemptions you want to use, either your particular state or the federal exemptions. With few exceptions, I advise people to use the federal exemptions due to the fact that you have the wildcard exemption available under the federal scheme, and most states don't have an equivalent exemption.

In the other states - Alabama, Arizona, California, Delaware, Florida, Georgia, Idaho, Illinois, Indiana, Iowa, Kansas, Louisiana, Maine, Maryland, Mississippi, Missouri, Montana, Nebraska, Nevada, North Carolina, North Dakota, New York, Ohio, Oklahoma, Oregon, South Carolina, South Dakota, Tennessee, Utah, Virginia, West Virginia, Wyoming – you can only use the state set of exemptions. The federal exemptions are not available to you.

Obviously, we aren't going to list the exemptions available for every state. But I will review how to apply the federal exemptions, and you can use this guide as a template for applying state exemptions if you live in a state where the federal ones aren't available. If you live in one of those states, simply Googling your state and "bankruptcy exemptions" (i.e. "California bankruptcy exemptions") will bring up websites where these exemptions are listed.

If you have equity in any property you own that you won't be able to exempt through this process, you probably have two options. First, you might pay the value of that non-exempt equity to the Trustee appointed in your case. The Trustee will take his or her share of that money and distribute the rest on a pro-rata basis to your creditors. The second option will be to turn over that property to the Trustee in your case. The Trustee will likely sell the property, pay you the value of any exemption you were able to apply to this property, and pay the rest to your creditors – after taking his cut. The point is, you should try to exempt all the equity you have in everything you own. Here's how you do it:

In Schedule C you address the exemption of property. Find Schedule C by going to

http://www.uscourts.gov/bkforms/bankruptcy_forms.html

and opening the form "B6C Schedule C - Property Claimed as Exempt." You will also need to have in front of you the Schedules A, B and D you filled out earlier. Immediately put your name and the name of your spouse on the line at the top left of the form next to "In re." Then, follow these steps:

1.   If you live in a state where you can use the federal exemptions and you intend to take this approach, check the first box on the top left of the form where it says "11 U.S.C. §522(b)(2)." If you cannot use the federal exemptions in your state, check the box just below that one where it says "11 U.S.C. §522(b)(3)."

2.   If you need additional pages to exempt all your property, go ahead and copy this page as many times as you need to.

3.   We'll take this one step at a time. First we'll look at Schedule A. If you don't own any real estate and have nothing listed on this schedule, go to paragraph 4. Otherwise:

    ♦ Look at the first piece of real estate listed on Schedule A. Copy the description of that real estate from the far left column in Schedule A into the far left column on the first available line in Schedule C.

    ♦ Next, list what law is providing you with the exemption. To get the relevant information, go to Appendix C in this book if you're using federal exemptions. If you're using state exemptions, refer to the state law citation for the exemption you're using. For example, if this is your home and you're using the federal exemptions, the federal exemption for your home would be listed as 11 U.S.C. §522(d)(1). If you don't know how to make the § mark that signifies "section" in the language of lawyers, use "sec." instead.

♦ Next, in the column on the far right, you will note the value of your equity in the property. Get that number from Schedule A by subtracting column five from column four (column 4 – column 5). If the resulting number is zero or less than zero, write 0 in columns three and four in this row of Schedule C, and then skip the next paragraph. Otherwise, write the resulting number on the far right column of this line and go on.

♦ Now you need to decide how you will exempt this property. Look in Appendix C of this book to see how much exemption is available for your asset under the exemption you listed in column two of Schedule C. For example, if this is your home, you're filing individually, you listed $9000 in column four of Schedule C, and you're using the homestead exemption from the federal exemptions (11 U.S.C. §522(d)(1) from column 2), then you will list $9000 in column three of Schedule C. Since that property is now fully exempt you can go on to the next paragraph. If, by contrast, you listed $21,000, you can only exempt $20,200 using the homestead exemption. There is $800 of remaining exemption. If that's the case, you need to find another exemption to cover the remaining $800. Such an exemption does exist. Remember the wildcard exemption? Most of the wildcard exemption only exists if you have up to $10,125 left from the homestead exemption. Obviously, you don't have that available here since you fully used the homestead exemption. Nevertheless, you still have $1075 of wildcard exemption available on top of that. You can use the wildcard exemption for any kind of property you want. Therefore, you can use the wildcard exemption to eat up the remaining equity you have in your home. Now you're finished and ready to move on to 3e. However, if you still have remaining equity that isn't exempted, you have a couple of options:

- Review the value you placed on the property, keeping in mind this is liquidation value, not what you paid for it. Especially in this economy, the value of real estate is low. Did you overvalue the property? If so, you may be able to adjust the value sufficiently to exempt the property.

- Make sure you're only listing the value you actually have in the equity of the property. For example, do you own this property jointly with someone else? If so, did you divide the value of the property by the number of the people who own the property, and then only list your share of the equity? For example, if you share the deed of your home with your two parents, the home is worth $100,000 and you have a mortgage on it for $70,000, even through there is $30,000 of equity in the home, your share of that equity is only $10,000.

- If you're filing jointly with your spouse, did you double the exemption? For example, if you and your spouse jointly own a home worth $100,000 with a mortgage on it for $70,000, you and your spouse could each use $15,000 of your homestead exemption and still have $6275 each in wildcard exemption available to you. That's $100,000 - $70,000 = $30,000 in equity, divided by 2 (for the two of you) = $15,000. The homestead exemption for each of you is worth $20,200, so $20,200 – 15,000 = $5200. Since $5200 is less than the $10,125 you're allowed to apply to the wildcard exemption, you can use all $5200 for the wildcard exemption. Then, the $5200 from the remaining homestead exemption + the $1075 of the wildcard exemption = $6275 remaining wildcard exemption for each of you.

- Be prepared to either write a check to the Trustee for the value of equity that isn't exempt to keep the property or be willing to have the Trustee sell the property. A final option is:

- Talk to a Bankruptcy attorney. A qualified Bankruptcy attorney might be able to suggest alternatives to help you through this process.

♦ On a separate sheet of paper, list all the exemptions you used in the last paragraph, if any, and note the amount of exemption you've used. You need to keep track of the remaining amounts available to you for each exemption. Once you've applied the homestead exemption, you need to take the remaining amount of homestead exemption up to $10,125 and add $1075 to that number so you can determine how much wildcard exemption is available to you for everything else. If you're filing jointly, make two columns on your sheet of paper: one for your exemptions, and one for your spouse's.

♦ Look back at Schedule A. Is any real estate remaining? If not, continue to paragraph 4 below. If yes, go back to the beginning of paragraph 3 above and list the next piece of real estate. Remember, you can only use the homestead exemption for your home, cemetery plot, or a manufactured home, condo or coop if that's where you live. Any investment properties, vacation properties or vacant land in which you have equity will need to be protected using any wildcard exemption you have available.

4.   Now that you've finished exempting your real estate (hopefully), we'll work to exempt your other assets. First, lay out Schedule B beside Schedule D. You'll need space for this. Next to that, lay out the list showing the amounts you've used from your exemptions. Finally, lay out the list of exemptions from Appendix C of this book, or the state exemptions you downloaded. You will refer to all these documents as you work through Schedule C.

a.   Look at Schedule B. For the first piece of property listed on Schedule B, write the description of the property from column 3 of Schedule B on column 1 of the next available line on Schedule C.

b.   Next, check the value of the property listed in column 5 of Schedule B. Before you do anything else, look at Schedule D to see if a lien is eating up equity of that property.

-    If yes, take the value of the property listed in column 5 of schedule B, minus the amount of the debt secured by this property listed in column 8 of Schedule D. If you have more than one loan secured by this property, also subtract the value of any other loans secured by this property from the value of the property. After you've subtracted all the loans from the value of the property, if the number is zero or negative, write zero in column three and four of that line on Schedule C. You're now finished with this piece of property. Go to 4e. If the resulting number is more than zero, write that number in column 4 of that line in Schedule C, then move on to 4c.

-    If there is no lien on that property, write the value of the property from column 5 of Schedule B in the line for that property in column 4 of Schedule C.

c.   Now it's time to decide how you'll exempt this property. Look at the value of the property and the exemptions available from Appendix C of this book or the state exemptions you downloaded. First, what exemption makes sense? There are specific exemptions for vehicles, household furnishings (furniture, household goods, clothing, appliances, books, animals, musical instruments), jewelry, tools you use for your work, term life insurance, cash-value life insurance, health aids, Social Security benefits, unemployment benefits, alimony or child support, and a 401K or IRA. Look at the exemptions and decide what works best for your specific property. Then notice the limits for each exemption. Some exemptions are unlimited, such as the 401K exemption, but most have a limit. Remember you have the wildcard exemption to help you exempt anything that doesn't otherwise qualify. Also, you can use more than one exemption to protect a specific piece of property. If you own a vehicle worth $5000, you can use the $3225 available to protect the vehicle, plus $1775 from the wildcard exemption. Once you've determined an approach to exempt a specific piece of property, move on.

d. Using the list from Appendix C or the state exemptions you downloaded, write the exemption you're using in column 2 of Schedule C on the line for that piece of property (i.e. 11 U.S.C. sec. 522(d)(5) for the federal wildcard exemption) and in column 3 of Schedule C, list the amount of the exemption you're using to protect that property. If you use more than one exemption to protect a specific piece of property (as in the car example from 4c), then list the second exemption under the first in the row for that piece of property in columns 2 and 3. Check to be sure the property is fully protected by adding the value of the exemptions in column 3 for that property. The value of the exemptions should equal the value of your piece of property listed in column 4. If you're unable to fully exempt the property, these are your options:

- Review the value you placed on the property. Remember to use liquidation value, not what you paid for it. Essentially, pretend you'll be selling the property in a garage sale or on eBay. Did you overvalue the property? If so, you may be able to adjust the value enough for an exemption to apply.

- Make sure you're only listing the value you actually have in the equity of the property. For example, do you own this property jointly with someone else? If so, did you divide the value of the property by the number of the people who own the property and only list your equity share? For example, suppose you're on the title of your car with your two parents. If the car is worth $10,000 and you have a loan on it for $4,000, even through the car's equity is $6,000, your share of that equity is only $2,000.

- If you're filing jointly with your spouse, did you double the exemption? For example, if you and your spouse jointly own a car worth $10,000 with a loan on it for $4,000. In that case, you and your spouse could each use $3,000 of your vehicle exemption and not have to use any of the wildcard exemption.

- Be prepared to either write a check to the Trustee for the value of the equity that is not exempt, or be willing to have the Trustee sell the property.

- A final option is to speak with a Bankruptcy attorney. A qualified Bankruptcy attorney may find alternatives to help you through this process.

e. On the list of exemptions you're using, note the exemptions you just used and their value. Remember, you have limited exemptions and once you run out of them, you can't use them again. Keep track.

f. Now that you've fully protected this piece of property, go back to Schedule B. Do you have any more property listed on that schedule? If yes, return to 4a. If not, you're finished. Move on.

Congratulations. Dealing with exemptions is the toughest part of this process. If you managed to exempt all your property, you're well on your way to completing this petition. If you ran into a brick wall here, you may have a case that's too complex to manage without the help of a Bankruptcy attorney.

You need to take one more step in order to keep the property you want. This is called the Statement of Intention, and it's easy compared to Schedule C.

To get to the Statement of Intention, return to

http://www.uscourts.gov/bkforms/bankruptcy_forms.html

and open the form "B8 Chapter 7 Individual Debtor's Statement of Intention." To complete this schedule, you need to refer to schedules C, D and G you've already completed. The purpose of this form is to inform the court, Trustee and your creditors what assets you want to keep, what assets have liens on them, and the contracts or leases you want to keep going.

Write your name on the top left of the first page of the form. If you're filing jointly, add your spouse's name. Now let's start with Schedule D.

1. Starting with the first creditor listed in Schedule D, write that creditor's name under "Creditor's Name" in the first available box on the Statement of Intent.

2. Under "Describe Property Securing Debt," write the description of the property from column 4 of Schedule D.

3. Then, check the box for:
    ♦ "Surrendered" – if you want to let the creditor have the property back and have no further liability to that creditor, or
    ♦ "Retained" – if you want to keep the property. Remember that if you want to keep this property, you will have to keep making payments on it.

4. For each item where you checked "Retained," check the box for "Reaffirm the debt." Anything else there will require an attorney's assistance.

5. Finally, if the property is fully exempted in Schedule C or the liens from Schedule D eat up all the equity in the property, check "Claimed as exempt." Otherwise, check "Not claimed as exempt."

6. Do you have any other secured debts listed in Schedule D? If yes, go back to 1. If no, you're finished with Part A. Note that the third page of this statement in the website is a continuation page you can copy and add to until you've addressed all the creditors listed in Schedule D.

Now we'll move on to leases and contracts. This is even easier than dealing with the creditors from Schedule D. In Part B of the Statement of Intention you'll address how you want the leases and contracts handled, starting on the second page of the statement and continuing on the third page (continuation sheet) if needed.

1. Look at Schedule G. If you have no leases or contracts listed, you're done. Date and sign this sheet at the bottom.

2. If you have leases and contracts listed on Schedule G, start with the first one listed. Write the name of the other party to the contract or lease in the first available box under "Lessor's name."

3. Under "Describe Leased Property:" do exactly that. What are you leasing? What is the contract for?

4. Next, do you want to keep the contract or lease going, or do you want to end it with no further liability to you?
    ♦ Check *yes* if you want to keep it going
    ♦ Check *no* if you want to get rid of it

5. Do you have any leases or contracts left on Schedule G? If yes, go back to item 2. If no, write the number of continuation sheets you used just below the boxes to the left, and date and sign the document.

You're done. Now we're ready to move on to the Statement of Financial

Affairs. This is the last major part of this petition you'll complete before it can be filed. You're making great progress!

Chapter 11

The Statement of Financial Affairs

Now we are going to address one of the most intimidating documents ever created by Congress and the bureaucrats in Washington. But in truth, it isn't all that bad. I'm going to walk you through the Statement of Financial Affairs.

This document can get complicated in a hurry if you have a difficult case. I'll help you fill out the portions of this document needed by 99 percent of those who fill it out. If you fall into the one percent category, you should be working with a Bankruptcy attorney.

Once again, go back to the website

http://www.uscourts.gov/bkforms/bankruptcy_forms.html

and open the form "B7 Statement of Financial Affairs." At the top left of the first page, write your name and your spouse's name if you're filing jointly next to "In re." Now, follow these steps.

1. Take out your tax returns for the past two years. For item 1 on the Statement, enter the gross wages you received for each year under "amount" (this will be located at the top of page one of your federal tax return). If you have business income, list the business income from the tax return under "amount." Next to the number, write the phrase "2009 (or whatever year applies) gross wages" under "Source." You will do this step for each of the past two years.

2. Next, go back to all your pay stubs. Take the last pay stub you (and your spouse if you have one) received from each job you had during the last calendar year. Under "amount" write your year-to-date gross wages from each job. Next to that number, under "source" write the phrase "2010 (or whatever year applies) year-to-date gross wages to (husband/wife) Debtor from (name of employer)." Take that step for every employer you had during the current calendar year.

3. Let's move on to item 2. This is where you list all other sources of income including Social Security, unemployment, child support, alimony, food stamps, pension, 401K withdrawals, etc. Check your tax returns for the past two years to see what other sources of income are listed besides wages. In item 2 on the statement, list the amount from the tax return under "amount" and the source of the income (Social Security, unemployment, child support, alimony, food stamps, pension, 401K withdrawals, etc.).

4. Get out your checkbook. Look through your check register and identify all payments to a single creditor amounting to $600 or more in the last three months. This could be three payments of $200 over the last three months to one creditor, but the payments must be to just one creditor. Once you've determined if you paid more than $600 in the last three months to a single creditor, for item 3a list the name and address of the creditor, the dates you made payments to that creditor, the total amount paid, and the amount you still owe. If you paid that creditor off, list zero under "amount still owing." You need to take this step for every creditor to whom you paid more than $600. Don't worry, this step will have no impact on you, but be prepared for the fact that you'll need to supply the Trustee with copies of checks or bank statements demonstrating you made these payments. If you haven't made any cumulative payments to a single creditor of more than $600 in the last three months, then check the box next to 3a under "None" and move on.

5. Check the box under "None" for 3b.

6. Next, ask yourself if you paid any relatives money you owed them during the last twelve months. If you did, the Trustee will probably go to your relatives to get these funds back. If you're thinking of paying back a relative now, don't do it. If you did pay back a relative, list the name and address of that relative under 3c, the date you made the payment, the amount you paid, and the amount you still owe. If you didn't pay money to relatives during last year (which is hopefully the case), check the box next to 3c under "None."

7. Next comes 4a. Have you been sued in the last year? If no, check the box next to 4a under "None" and move on. If yes, write the caption and the case number (this would be on the documents you received in the case, i.e. "Citibank USA v. John Q. Sample, Case No. 09-12345). Next to that, write the type of lawsuit. The most common will be either "collections action" if this is a case where someone is trying to collect a debt from you, or "divorce action" if you're getting divorced. Next to that, write the name of the

court where this case is happening. You'll find that information on documents from the lawsuit, i.e. "Macomb County Circuit Court"), and the status (either "pending" or "judgment entered" if there is already a judgment). Enter this information for every lawsuit with which you've been involved during the last year.

8. Have you been garnished or had property seized in the last year? Note this question does not include a repo by a car or boat lender, or a foreclosure. We will get to that next. However, if a credit card lender or other creditor sued you and had the sheriff seize your vehicle, then list that seizure here. If the answer is no, check the box next to 4b under "none" and move on. If yes, write the name and address of the creditor who seized the property, the date the property was seized, and the amount of money garnished from you or the kind of property that was seized (i.e. "car seized.") Enter this information for each creditor who took money or property from you in the last year.

9. Next, we will deal with repos and foreclosures, as well as where you might have "returned" a vehicle you were leasing, turned in property you owed money on, or did a "deed in lieu of foreclosure" for a house. If none of those things have happened in the last year, check the box next to item 5 under "none" and move on. If you've had any of those things happen during the year, you need to report it here. First, list the name and address of the creditor who got its collateral back. Next, write the date this happened. Lastly, list an approximate value for the property. Do this for every repossession, foreclosure, or return that happened in the last year, and then move on.

10. Unless you're an unusual person, check the two boxes for item 6 under "None" and move on.

11. Have you made any gifts or charitable contributions of more than $100 in the last year (not including normal Christmas and birthday gifts to family members less than $200 per person)? This could be charitable contributions such as giving $10 per week at church. Don't worry about clothing donations to the Salvation Army (believe me, even though they let you take a hefty tax deduction, the clothes aren't worth more than $100 for our purposes). If no, check the box under "None" next to item 7 and move on. If yes, write the name and address of the person or charity you gave the money to. If the person is a relative, write how you're related to that person (i.e. "Debtor's father"). Otherwise write "none" under "Relationship to Debtor." Next, write the date you made the gift. If you made charitable contributions to your church each week, write

"weekly." Finally, write the approximate value of the gift, or the approximate amount of money you contributed. Write a line like this for each charity or person to whom you gave more than $100 in the last year.

12. Have you had any losses from fire, casualty, theft, or gambling in the last year? If no, check the box under "None" next to item 8. If yes, describe the property you lost and its value. For gambling losses, even if they were lost at different casinos at different times, write the total amount of your gambling losses under "Description and Value of Property." Next, describe what happened. You don't need to go into detail. Appropriate explanations would include "gambling losses," "car accident, received $1000 from insurance company," or "basement flooded, not covered by insurance." Lastly, write the date the loss occurred. Fill out a line for each kind of loss you've incurred over the last twelve months.

13. Have you paid anyone to help deal with your debts? You should disclose those payments in item 9. This could be credit counseling, debt consolidation, foreclosure assistance, or money paid to a Bankruptcy attorney. Be sure to include the payments you made for the required Bankruptcy credit counseling. For each kind of assistance you paid for in the last year, write the name and address of the person or company you paid, the date of the payment, and the amount of money you paid.

14. Have you sold, given away, or otherwise transferred any property (including personal property such as cars and boats) during the past two years? If no, check the box "None" next to item 10a. If yes, write the name and address of the person or company to whom you transferred the property, the date of the transfer, the kind of property you transferred, and what you received in return. Be aware of the fact that if you gave away something to a relative, the Trustee can get that property back and distribute it to your creditors. Also be aware that payment for the property could be in the form of something other than money. For example, you might have transferred a vehicle to your son or daughter in exchange for doing work around your house, childcare, or some other service. If you believe you received some type of "value" in exchange for the property you transferred, then there's nothing wrong with the transfer. Just make sure you disclose on this form the value of what you received. Do this for every transfer of property during the last two years.

15. Check the box under "None" next to 10b. If you have a trust you've transferred assets into, you should be talking to an attorney.

16. Have you closed any bank accounts or other financial accounts

(including 401Ks or IRAs) in the past year? If no, check the box under "None" next to item 11. If yes, write the name and address of the bank or financial institution where you closed the account. Then write what kind of account it was (i.e. checking, savings, 401K, IRA, etc.) the last four digits of the account number (if you don't know the last four digits, put the last four digits of your Social Security number), and the amount of money in the account when you closed it. Lastly, write the date you closed the account on the far right. Go through this step for every account you closed in the last year.

17. Do you have a safe deposit box, or have you had one in the last year? If no, check the box under "None" next to item 12 and move on. If yes, write the name and address of the bank where the safe deposit box is located, the name and address of everyone with access to the safe deposit box, a description of the contents of the box, and the date the box was closed if it's no longer in your possession. Make sure any property contained in the box is listed in Schedule B and exempted on Schedule C. If the box just contains documents such as a will and a passport, make that clear by listing these items.

18. A setoff is where you have a bank account and a debt with the same bank. Because of that, the bank takes money from your bank account without your permission to apply those funds to your debt. Did that happen to you in the last three months? If no, check the box under "None" next to item 13. If yes, write the name and address of the bank, the date it happened, and the amount they took from you.

19. Do you have any property in your possession that belongs to someone else? This may include a bank account for your children with your name on it. If no, check the box under "None" next to item 14. If yes, write the name and address of the owner of the property. If the owner is a minor child, write "minor child daughter" or "minor child son" – you do not want to list contact information of minors – a description of the property and its value (i.e. minor bank account, $100), and where the property is located. Complete this step for each kind of property you have that belongs to someone else.

20. Have you lived at the same address for more than three years? If yes, check the box under "None" next to item 15. If no, write each prior address during the past three years, the name you used while living there (i.e. might have been before you were married), and the dates you lived there. Add that information for every address during the last three years.

21. In the last eight years, have you lived in one of the following states: Alaska, Arizona, California, Idaho, Louisiana, Nevada, New Mexico, Puerto Rico, Texas, Washington, or Wisconsin? If no, check the box under "None" next to item 16. If yes, do you have any spouses you were married to who aren't listed on your petition (i.e. you're filing individually and are married, or you were divorced)? If no, check the box for "None" for item 16. If yes, write the name of every spouse in one of those states during the last eight years.

22. I'm guessing you aren't a big polluter with environmental judgments against you. If you are, you should talk to a lawyer. Otherwise, just check the boxes under "None" next to items 17a, b and c.

23. We're almost there! In the last six years, have you owned or operated a business of which you owned more than five percent? This could include self-employment. If no, check the box next to item 18. If yes, write the name of the business (if it's self-employment, write that), the last four digits of your Social Security number, or the business's taxpayer ID number if it had one, the address of the business, what the business did, and the beginning and ending dates (if it's no longer operating) of the business. Write this information for any business you owned more than five percent of in the last six years.

24. Were any of the businesses listed in item 23 considered single-asset real estate businesses? Those are businesses where the entire business consists of owning a piece of property and renting it out. If no, check the box under "None" next to 18b. If yes, write the name of the business and the address of the real estate it owns.

Since this book is designed for individuals rather than business owners, I won't address the other questions in the Statement of Financial Affairs. These questions are for businesses or people who own businesses. If these questions apply to you, then go through the remaining questions. If not, check the boxes under "None" for questions 19 through 26. Then, at the end of the statement, sign and date the document. You're done. Let's finish up now.

Chapter 12

Finishing up – The Summary of Schedules,
Matrix, Declaration Concerning Debtor's Schedules,
Statement of Social Security Numbers, and the Filing Fee

W e need to take a few final steps to get these documents ready to file. By the end of this chapter, your case will be filed.

The Summary of Schedules: This is the first document we'll deal with in this chapter. To get the document, go back to the website

http://www.uscourts.gov/bkforms/bankruptcy_forms.html

and open the document "B6 Summary of Schedules (Includes Statistical Summary of Certain Liabilities)." On the top left of the page next to "In re," write your name. If you're filing jointly, add your spouse's name. On the top right of the page next to Chapter, write the number 7.

We're now going to fill out the table. Under the column for "Attached (yes/no)," write *Yes* in each box. Now, put in front of you all the schedules we filled out earlier. Count how many sheets make up your Schedule A. Write that number under "No. of sheets." Do the same thing for each schedule listed on the left of the table.

Next, look at your Schedule A and check the last page. At the bottom of the page is a box you filled in for Total. Put that number in the box under Assets for Schedule A. Now, do the same thing for Schedule B, where you'll find the Total box at the bottom right of the last page of the Schedule. Now add the two numbers you listed under Assets in the Summary of Schedules and put that number in the Total box at the bottom of the Assets column.

Next, turn to Schedule D. On the last page, at the bottom of the eighth column, is a Total box. Write the amount from that box in the box for Schedule D in the Liabilities column on the Summary of Schedules. Next, from Schedule E, take the total from the box at the bottom of column 8 and write that total in the box for Schedule E under Liabilities. Next, from the last page of Schedule F, take the Total number from the bottom of the last column and put that number in the box for Schedule F in the

Liabilities column. Now add the three boxes in the Liabilities column and put that number at the bottom Total box.

Now, get your Schedule I. Take the total from the bottom – line 16 – and put that number in the box in the Other column for Schedule I. Next, from Schedule J, take the number from line 18 (the line with a dark box around the number) and write that number in the box under the "Other" column for Schedule J at the bottom right of the table. You're done with this page. Move on to page 2.

This page is called the "Statistical Summary of Certain Liabilities and Related Data." As usual, at the top left of the page next to "In re," write your name and add the name of your spouse, if you're filing jointly. On the top right of the page next to Chapter, write the number "7."

First we'll fill out the "Type of Liability" box. Take out your Schedule E. Do you owe any Domestic Support Obligations? If no, write the number "0" in the top right hand box of this table. If yes, get the total of your domestic support obligations from the Subtotal box at the bottom of column 8 of the domestic support obligations page and write that number in the top right box of this table.

Next, do you owe any taxes? If no, write the number "0" in the second right hand box of this table. If yes, get the total of your taxes from the Subtotal box at the bottom of column 8 of the taxes page. Write that number in the second right box of this table.

Next, do you have debts arising from claims that resulted from driving while intoxicated? If no, write the number "0" in the third right hand box of this table. If yes, get the total of this kind of debt from the Subtotal box at the bottom of column 8 of the page for this kind of debt. Write that number in the third right box of this table.

Now, get out your Schedule F. Remember that student loans are non-dischargeable in Bankruptcy. Therefore, you'll need to list a total for those debts. If you don't have any student loans, write "0" in the fourth box in the right-hand column. If you do, you'll have to go through the pages of Schedule F, and every time you see a student loan debt, add the total for that debt. Once you've added the totals for all student loan debts, put that total in the fourth box in the right hand column. Now, put the number "0" in the next two boxes in the right-hand column of this table. Add all the numbers in the right-hand column of this table and put the total in the bottom box of that column.

Let's move on to the second table. From Schedule I, put the number from line 16 in the first box in the right-hand column of this table. In the second box at the right of this table, write the number from Schedule J, line 18. Now, turn to the Means Test. Get the number from Line 12 of the Means Test and put that number in the bottom right box of that table.

Last table. Get your Schedule D out. Look at the last page of that schedule. From the very bottom right hand box of that schedule, get the number you'll write in the top right box of the last table. Next, from the last page of Schedule E, get the number from the bottom box of column 9. Put that number in the only box in the middle column of this table. In the third box down on the right-hand column of this table, write "0." Now, go back to the "Summary of Schedules," the first page of this document, and get the number from the box in the Liabilities column for Schedule F. Write that number in the fourth box in the right-hand column of the table we're working on. Last step: Add the numbers in the far right-hand column of this table and write that number in the bottom right box.

The Matrix: This section is a pain, but it isn't difficult. Get out all your schedules, because we need to make sure everyone who has an interest in your case will be notified. You need to go through Schedules D, E, F, G and H and type the name and address of everyone on those schedules. Do this in paragraph form, separated by a blank line. The result should look something like this:

```
Accurate Account Solutions, LLC
Collections
PO Box 244
Clarkston, MI 48347

Afni, Inc.
404 Brock Drive
PO Box 427
Bloomington, IL 61702-3427

Arrow Financial Services
5996 W Touhy Ave
Niles, IL 60714

Capital 1 Bank
Attn: C/O TSYS Debt Management
Po Box 5155
Norcross, GA 30091
```

The page should be blank otherwise. If a creditor is listed more than once in your schedules, you need only list them once in the matrix. Make sure all your creditors are accounted for, because if they aren't listed, the debt may not be discharged. Once you've listed all the creditors, add your own name and address: you want to get notices of everything in your case. Once you've done that, print the sheets and you're done.

The Declaration Concerning Debtor's Schedules: From the website

http://www.uscourts.gov/bkforms/bankruptcy_forms.html

open the form "B6 Declaration Concerning Debtor's Schedules." This is the easiest form yet. Write your name and your spouse's name, if you're filing jointly, at the top left of the form next to "In re." You and your spouse, if you're filing jointly, need to date and sign the form at the top. That's it.

The Statement of Social Security Number(s): This is another easy form. From the website

http://www.uscourts.gov/bkforms/bankruptcy_forms.html

open the form "B21 Statement of Social Security Number." At the top left of the page, next to "In re," write your name and the name of your spouse, if you're filing jointly. Below that, next to "Address" write your address. Below that, under "Last four digits of Social-Security or Individual Taxpayer-Identification No," write the last four digits of your Social Security number and the last four of your spouse's Social Security number if you're filing jointly. Below that, next to "1. Name of Debtor" write your full legal name with your last name first. Under that, check the first box and type your full Social Security number in the space provided. If you're filing jointly, write your spouse's full legal name with last name first next to "2. Name of Joint Debtor." Again, check the box under that one and write your spouse's full Social Security number in the blank space. Then you and your spouse (if you're filing jointly) sign and date this document at the bottom of the page.

You should know this document is not part of the public file in the Bankruptcy case. The court is concerned about identity theft, so this form is not disclosed. You can feel comfortable putting your Social Security numbers here.

The Filing Fee: Now for the bad news. There is a fee of $299 to file Chapter 7. You have three ways to deal with this fee:

1. Pay it when you bring in your petition. Bring a check made out to "Bankruptcy Clerk" for the full amount. You're on your way!
2. Ask the court to allow you to make payments. Go to the website

http://www.uscourts.gov/bkforms/bankruptcy_forms.html

and open the form "B3A Application and Order to Pay Filing Fee in Installments." The form is self-explanatory. You propose a payment plan to pay the $299. Typically, if the plan is reasonable, it will be approved. If you propose a payment at the time of filing, bring in a check for that amount when you file your case. Bring this completed and signed form with you when you bring in the other documents for filing. Know that if you miss a payment, your case will probably be dismissed and you'll go back to square one.

3. If you truly cannot afford the filing fee, you can ask the court to excuse the filing fee in its entirety. To do so, go back to the website http://www.uscourts.gov/bkforms/bankruptcy_forms.html

and open the form "B3B Application for Waiver of Chapter 7 Filing Fee." Again, the form is self-explanatory and requires you to explain to the court why you can't afford to make these payments at all. Fill out this form in its entirety, sign it, and bring it with you when you file your documents with the court. Know that if your circumstances change, the court can revoke this permission.

Filing the Case: You're done! Congratulations. You've completed all the forms required to file your Chapter 7 Bankruptcy case. All you need to do now is make 4 copies of the documents and bring the entire package to the Bankruptcy clerk's office for your district. Make sure you keep one copy for your records. If you don't know the district you're in, go to the following website,

http://www.justice.gov/ust/eo/bapcpa/ccde/states.htm,

select your state, then look for your county to find out your district. The U.S. Courts website is very helpful as well. You can go to this website

http://www.uscourts.gov/courtlinks/,

click "Bankruptcy Court," enter your zip code, then hit "Search." The Bankruptcy Courts for your area will immediately pop up, giving you an address and a map to the court. This is where you go during business hours to file your petition.

Chapter 13

The Automatic Stay

*I*f you're like most of my clients, you've been dealing with creditors who call you day in and day out, burning up your phone lines from early in the morning until late at night. I'm sure you've been receiving threatening messages, letters, and even lawsuits. Perhaps your wages have been garnished. Here's the good news. Now that you've filed Bankruptcy, that all stops. Immediately. You can answer the phone and tell your creditors you filed Bankruptcy, give them the case number the clerk gave you, and then hang up. They can't call you after that. If you don't want to talk with them, don't. They will receive notice from the court of your Bankruptcy filing in a matter of days. Remember the matrix we wrote, listing all your creditors? Again, from that point on, they can't call you.

This is called the Automatic Stay, one of the best laws ever passed by the Federal Government. The theory is, we want all your creditors to come to the Bankruptcy Court and have their claims decided by the court. Congress didn't want your creditors trying to back-door you to get more from you than they're entitled to in Bankruptcy Court. The law provides for substantial penalties if a creditor doesn't comply with this stay. If a creditor harms you in some way after the case has been filed, you can sue for damages, legal fees and even additional damages to punish them. If you're the victim of such a violation, you might want to visit a Bankruptcy attorney. An attorney may take the case on the basis of fees from the damages you're entitled to. However, most creditors back off as soon as they hear Bankruptcy: they know the kind of trouble they can get into.

A few exceptions to the Automatic Stay may impact you. First is the set-off, a process we discussed earlier. When you have both a bank account and a debt with the same bank, the bank can take funds directly from your account to cover the debt. Banks can do this, because while you owe a debt to the bank or credit union, the bank owes you a debt in the form of the bank account. As a result, with a set-off, they're just evening up the accounts. That's the theory. The net result is pretty nasty when you have funds taken right out of your bank account. As a result, for my clients who owe a debt to the bank or credit union where they do their banking, I always advise them to immediately open an account at a bank where they have no debts and remove their funds from the old bank account as soon as possible. Don't forget to stop all deposits into that old bank account. The bank will grab those funds and you could be damaged, with no recourse.

The other important exception to the Automatic Stay involves child support and other domestic support obligations. If you have funds taken periodically out of your paycheck for child support, that deduction will continue, even though you filed Bankruptcy.

You should be aware of one practical effect of the Automatic Stay. If you have a mortgage payment, car loan payment, car lease payment, a boat loan, or rent for your home, due to the Automatic Stay you won't receive statements from those creditors while your case is pending. That's because the Automatic Stay prevents any creditors from trying to collect from you. If you intend to keep the collateral secured by a loan, you still need to make those payments. Just because you don't get a statement doesn't mean you shouldn't keep paying. Keep making the same payment you always make to the same place, at the same time. If you want to keep the stuff, you need to stay current. You might even want to mark your calendar to make sure you send payments as scheduled. Now that you're in Bankruptcy, the creditor will move quickly if you fall behind. Don't worry, once your case is over, you'll start receiving the statements again.

Stop paying your other creditors. Don't pay on credit cards, medical bills or any other debts that will be discharged in your case. If you're being garnished, call the attorney who's garnishing you to tell them about your Bankruptcy. It's up to them to stop the garnishment at that point – and fast. If you're being sued, notify the attorney who's suing you. If you've made any agreements for payment on your debts, stop paying on that as well. This is the whole point of Bankruptcy.

As a result of the Automatic Stay, it almost feels as if your case is immediately over. Unfortunately, your case is just beginning. You need to take certain steps to ensure you get your discharge and the fresh start this process is all about.

Chapter 14

Next Steps

Within a few days after you file, you'll receive a notice from the court telling you a number of important things. First, your case number will be listed on this document. Next, your Trustee will be listed. The date of your hearing, the "First Meeting of Creditors" or as Bankruptcy attorneys refer to it, the "341 hearing," will also be on this paper. The document will list deadlines before which your creditors need to take action if they want to stop your Bankruptcy from proceeding, and it informs creditors of the kinds of actions they cannot take now that you've filed Bankruptcy. Keep this document handy. If a creditor wants documentation about your Bankruptcy filing, this is what you'll send.

Now that you have this document in hand, you need to take a few steps to prepare for the hearing. The Trustee's name and address are on this document. Immediately send your Trustee copies of the following documents (Do NOT send originals):

1. The last two years' tax returns – these are the actual returns where you listed all your income and deductions you filed with the State and IRS, not just the 1099s and W2s employers sent you.

2. Pay stubs for all your jobs and your spouse's jobs for the last two months. If you do not receive pay stubs, you need to provide some proof of income. For example, if you receive Social Security or a pension, you send a statement showing your monthly payment. If these payments are direct-deposited into your bank account, bank statements will do. If you're self-employed, you need to provide bank statements for your business accounts showing deposits you've made from your work.

3. Bank statements for all your bank accounts for the past six months. Statements printed from the bank's website are fine.

4. Titles to all your vehicles and boats – unless you live in a state where the creditor holds onto the titles until the vehicles are paid off.

5. Copies of recorded mortgages and deeds to your home and any other real estate you own. Just so you know, you won't have these documents. I guarantee it. Even if you have the thick package they give you at closing, these documents won't be in there. You need to go to the county offices for the county in which your real estate is located. Find the Register of Deeds office and have the staff print copies of the recorded deed and recorded mortgages for all your real estate. If more than one are available, you want the most current deed, and the most current mortgages for each mortgage on the property (i.e. one for the first mortgage, one for the home equity loan, etc.). The mortgages are long documents, often running twenty-five or more pages. All you need are the first three pages and the signature page from each of them. Limiting the number of pages will reduce your copying expense.

6. Copies of recent statements from all 401K, IRA, and other brokerage accounts.

7. Copies of statements from any "cash value" or "whole life" life insurance policies.

Package up these documents and send them to the Trustee's office, along with a letter stating your case number and the date and time of your hearing. You need to get these documents to the Trustee at least two weeks before your hearing. The more documents you send to your Trustee and the earlier they arrive, the more smoothly your hearing will go. If you don't get these documents in on time, your case could be dismissed.

For the hearing itself you need a picture ID and Social Security card for both you and your spouse (if you're filing jointly). If you don't have these IDs with you, the Trustee will not hold your hearing and you'll have to come back a second time. Check to make sure you have both these documents. If not, get them. You can order a new Social Security card by going to a Social Security Administration office. You can find the nearest Social Security office by going to this website,

https://secure.ssa.gov/apps6z/FOLO/fo001.jsp,

entering your zip code and hitting "Locate." You can also order a Social Security card online at the following website:

http://www.ssa.gov/ssnumber/.

If you go in person to the Social Security Administration office, they can give you a print-out right then and there to satisfy the Social Security card requirement. Note the print-out has two pages, and you'll need to bring both of them to your hearing as a replacement for your card. For the picture ID, a driver's license, passport, or other State ID with your picture on it will work. Again, make sure you have these documents so you don't end up looking for them at the last minute.

Chapter 15

Can I Keep My Stuff In Bankruptcy?
Reaffirmations, Redemptions and Lease Assumptions

Most of my clients are concerned about losing property that's valuable to them as they go through this process. We've already discussed the process of exempting property from the Trustee on Schedule C, and the process of informing creditors of your intentions on the Statement of Intention. Now we'll discuss the final steps to keeping property that either has a lien attached to it securing one of your debts, or is the subject of a lease or contract.

You probably remember when we completed Schedule D that we described certain kinds of debts as "secured" debts. These debts include mortgages, home equity loans, car loans, boat loans, and other consumer loans. When we completed Schedule G, we also listed certain kinds of on-going leases or contracts. Then, on the Statement of Intent, we had to notify the Trustee and the other creditors whether you wanted to keep this property if doing so meant you would keep paying on these loans, leases, or contracts. Remember, you don't get to keep this kind of property unless you keep paying the creditors. And you need to take an additional step.

There are three ways you can keep property of the types we just listed. Stating your intentions in the Statement of Intent isn't enough. You need to execute certain documents and get them filed with the court. Then you can be secure in your ability to keep your property.

The first kind of document is called a Reaffirmation Agreement. This is a long and complicated document you must complete and file with the court. Typically, the creditor will send a form with blank spaces for you to complete and sign. Sometimes you need to contact the creditor directly and ask them to send you the reaffirmation agreement. Because you aren't represented by an attorney in this process, the creditor will take care of filing the document with the court – but this isn't automatic, so you need to make sure this step is followed. When completing the reaffirmation agreement, you'll find a section requiring you to disclose your income and expenses. Then you must subtract your expenses from income to show you have enough funds available to make the payments required under the reaffirmation agreement. To get these numbers, go back to your schedules I and J. The income will be the final number from line 16 on schedule I. The expenses will be the final number in line 18 of schedule J, minus the amount of the payment if you included that payment in your expenses for schedule J. You don't want to double-count this payment by including it in the expenses from schedule J and having that expense as an additional expense in the reaffirmation agreement. If you've done this correctly, unless you're in drastic financial trouble, you should have enough money left there to make the payment on this debt.

Because you aren't represented by an attorney, the court will typically set a hearing on this Reaffirmation Agreement. The judge will expect you to come to the courtroom (note this is not the Trustee, and the courtroom is not where the Trustees typically hold their hearings). The judge needs to make sure you understand the ramifications of the Reaffirmation Agreement – in particular the fact that this debt will not be discharged, and that if you don't make payments down the road the creditor can chase you to collect any funds owed. The judge will also point out that you have a period to rescind this agreement if you want to change your mind.

If you didn't have enough money to make these payments when you completed the income and expense part of the Reaffirmation Agreement, the judge will determine to her satisfaction if you're able to make these payments going forward. If the judge decides you can't make these payments, then she can refuse to approve the Reaffirmation Agreement, and you'll have to give back the property. This shows how careful you need to be when completing schedules I, J, and the income and expense portion of the Reaffirmation Agreement form.

Some creditors will trick you. You may believe the credit card you received from some jewelry store, a furniture store, or an electronics store like Best Buy or Dell, is unsecured debt, a credit card like any other. But then you receive in the mail a proposed Reaffirmation Agreement asking you to agree to continue making payments on the debt if you want to keep the property you purchased from them. Sellers of consumer goods can retain a lien in the property they sell you, sometimes unbeknownst to you. My suggestion is simple: if the collateral is jewelry and you want to keep the jewelry, you'll need to sign the agreement and go through the reaffirmation process. If the collateral is any other kind, like furniture, a computer, electronics, even eyeglasses – just ignore it. My experience has been that the creditor won't go through the process to come after the property, and even if they do, you can probably make a deal with them down the road. They don't want the collateral, it would cost them too much money to get it back, and it isn't worth selling. Jewelry is the one exception to that rule.

Sometimes creditors will offer a deal to reaffirm the debt. Most of the time such offers are made by creditors whose reaffirmation you should just throw out. For a furniture company or an electronics store, it doesn't matter what deal they're offering – you shouldn't reaffirm the debt. The good news comes from certain car lenders. I'm not talking about GMAC or Ford Motor Credit, but if you have a different kind of lender, often the kind who lends for the purposes of purchasing used vehicles, I often see them reduce your interest rate, reduce the total due, and reduce your payment to get you to keep paying on the vehicle. If the creditor is proposing a deal like this, the new terms of the loan will be listed in the Reaffirmation Agreement. Unfortunately, if you don't see such a change in the proposed reaffirmation, you probably won't get one. All you can do is keep your fingers crossed.

The last kind of creditor who'll send you a Reaffirmation Agreement is the credit union. Credit unions typically take the position that if you cause them a loss, they no longer allow you to be a member. You may have been a member of your credit union for a long time and would like to keep your account there. If that's the case, your credit union will probably allow you to reaffirm any debts you have with them. I suggest you be clear-eyed when you consider this Reaffirmation Agreement. If you owe the credit union a substantial amount of debt, like more than $1000, then just walk away. Ultimately, they are just a bank and plenty of banks are out there. If you owe the credit union less than $1000, it might be worth considering, since reaffirming this debt and continuing to make your payments with the credit union will help your credit score bounce back.

Lease assumption agreements are the next most common kind of document you may come across in this process. If you're leasing a vehicle with GMAC, Ford Motor Credit, or virtually any other lessor, they will send you a lease assumption agreement. This document is shorter and easier to deal with than the reaffirmation. Typically, it just requires your signature, and usually the judge won't set up a hearing to review it. If you get one of these documents and want to keep the lease going, sign the documents and send them back to the creditor for filing.

The last approach to discuss here is the redemption. If you're representing yourself in this process, the redemption may be too much for you to deal with. A redemption is where you pay off a vehicle, boat, or other personal property (note, this doesn't work with real estate) at the value of the property, not the amount you owe on it. So if you have a vehicle that's worth $3000 and you still owe $10,000, with a redemption you can pay $3000 and keep the vehicle. Sounds great, but you need to come up with the $3000 in one lump sum. You also need to file a motion with the court to get an order approving the redemption. Some creditors may finance the lower amount and they might assist you in preparing the documents required. To find them, Google "redemption funding" or "chapter 7 redemption."

Chapter 16

The First Meeting of Creditors

*T*his is the day of your hearing. In most Chapter 7 cases, unless you have to go in front of the judge for Reaffirmation Agreements, this will be your only hearing. You will be scared that day, as everyone is, but if you've taken the steps listed in this book you have nothing to worry about.

Typically, the day of a Trustee's hearings is divided into hour or half-hour blocks. Your hearing will be held sometime during that block. As a result, assuming the session runs more or less on time, you should be out of there within an hour.

You and your spouse are both required to attend if you're filing jointly. Certain exceptions to this rule exist, but they require court approval and you'll need a qualified Bankruptcy attorney to assist you. Keep in mind, this hearing is not optional.

Remember to bring your picture IDs and Social Security cards to the hearing. The Trustee will not hold your hearing without them. Also bring a copy of your signed petition and a copy of the documents you sent the Trustee. If a problem arises, you will want to have those documents with you.

If your Bankruptcy court is anything like ours, the hearing room is a circus, with people coming and going all the time. In the waiting area debtors represented by attorneys will meet their lawyers. Since you aren't one of them, you need to identify the room where your Trustee is holding his hearings. If more than one Trustee is holding hearings that day, you can identify your hearing room by the notices posted by the door.

Enter the hearing room. I know it seems strange, since the Trustee will be holding a hearing, but you'll see that people are constantly coming in and out of the room. Sit down. You will now wait for your case to be called.

You should know that some Trustees have a questionnaire they want you to fill out before your hearing. If they do, the questionnaire will be on the table. Get the questionnaire before your hearing and hand it to the

Trustee with your ID when your case is called. Having the questionnaire filled out often makes your hearing go a little faster.

When your turn comes, the Trustee will call your case (i.e. "calling case no. 10-12345, James and Julia Sample"). You're in a large conference room with a big conference table. Other people are sitting in the room, but they're all in your situation: people waiting for their cases to be called. When your case is called, go to the table and give the Trustee your ID. Typically, the Trustee will want you to remain standing. Since this is a court hearing, the Trustee will swear you in ("do you swear or affirm to tell the truth" or something to that effect). Once you've been sworn in, you can take your seats at the table.

Once you've been sworn in, the Trustee will probably want to see the copy of the petition you brought with you. Once he has looked at it, the Trustee will want you to verify on the record that the signatures on the petition are actually your signatures and that you read and reviewed these documents before you signed them. Then your hearing gets started.

The first thing the Trustee will do is defer to any creditors who showed up to the hearing. You should know it's rare for a creditor to show up to a hearing. The creditor is also expected to maintain a certain decorum in the hearing. This is not a place to yell at you, berate you, or make you feel bad. This is a place to ask you questions under oath. Just answer the questions, then move on.

Once any creditors are finished, the Trustee will ask questions that mirror the information you filled out in your schedules. If your schedules are properly completed, the Trustee will verify that information and complete your hearing. The typical hearing only lasts five to ten minutes, if everything is done correctly ahead of time,

If the Trustee wants additional documentation, he or she will typically give you a deadline to obtain that information. If you get the information to the Trustee in time, you probably won't have to go back to court. Ask the Trustee to clarify if you need to go back if additional documents are requested.

Keep these hints in mind while you're testifying:

1. You cannot help yourself in this hearing. You can only hurt yourself. Nevertheless, you need to go and cooperate. The goal, then, should be to get through the hearing saying as little as possible. You need to answer the questions, but "yes" and "no" should be your preferred answers. Do not go into explanations or justifications here. You will only hurt yourself. Remember that even though the Trustee may be nice, he or she is your opponent in this process.

2. The hearing will be recorded. As a result, you need to answer orally. Nodding your head, shaking your head, saying "uh-uh" will not work. You need to answer clearly so the tape machine can pick it up.

3. If you filed a joint case, you both need to answer all the questions. It may seem strange, but it isn't enough for just one of you to answer. Unless a question is specifically directed at one of you, both of you should answer.

Follow these simple steps and your hearing should be a success. The people who get into trouble are those who don't make the proper preparations or talk too much at the hearings. Do what you're supposed to, nothing more, nothing less, tell the truth at all costs, and you will be fine.

Chapter 17

The Discharge

After your hearing, there is usually a two-month waiting period to see if any creditors have issues with your case. These problems will have to be legal in nature. Saying "we want to be paid" isn't enough. Everyone wants to be paid: they just don't get to.

During this waiting period you'll also take care of the reaffirmation and lease assumption agreements. You need to handle these before your discharge or they won't take effect.

This is also the period during which you need to complete your second credit counseling. You have forty-five days from the hearing to get it done, but I suggest you complete this step as quickly as possible. Once you get the certificate of completion, file it with the court. Some courts require you to file an additional document with that certification. If so, you'll be able to get that document from the clerk's office.

If the waiting period goes by, no creditors rear their ugly heads, and you took all the necessary steps, you will get your discharge. This is one of the most anti-climactic moments you can imagine. After so much work, effort, and worry, you will get a one-page letter from the court saying something to the effect of "it appearing that you are entitled to a discharge, your discharge is hereby granted." The judges don't even sign the letter. Usually their signature is represented by a "/s/ judge's name" since most of the documents are computer-created.

Despite the fact that the letter seems unimpressive, it's one of the most valuable documents you will ever get, and you should keep it with your important papers. The discharge is a court order, an "injunction," that states all your creditors from before the time you filed Bankruptcy can no longer attempt to collect on your debts. If a creditor ever comes after you in the future on one of those debts, all you have to do is show them the discharge.

If, despite knowing about the discharge, a creditor continues to pursue collection of your debt, consider hiring a local Bankruptcy attorney. Such a violation could result in sanctions against the creditor, and those sanctions would pay the attorney's fee. Therefore, an attorney may agree to pursue an action against a creditor who continues harassing you.

Despite the fact that the discharge results in the forgiveness of your debts, federal law is clear that reducing the value of your debts does not constitute taxable income. This rule is a big benefit to you, since settling debts outside of Bankruptcy Court will result in additional taxes you owe. Not so with Bankruptcy. The discharge does not impact your taxes. Essentially the discharge allows you to get rid of your debts scot-free.

Chapter 18

Lawsuits in Bankruptcy, Preferences,
Fraudulent Conveyances,
Non-dischargeability Actions

*B*ecause so much of Bankruptcy is cordial and resolutions are worked out by negotiation rather than litigation, we sometimes forget this is an adversarial process. It is you against your creditors, and the court is there to settle the score if you can't come to some kind of resolution.

The number of attorneys who have actually litigated lawsuits in the Bankruptcy Court is small, but such lawsuits do happen. If you get involved in one, you'll probably need an attorney. This is not the time to go your own way. The good news is that many courts will appoint attorneys to represent you on a pro bono (for free) basis when you face this kind of lawsuit.

If you're served with one of these lawsuits, the most important thing is to respond. If you don't respond, the plaintiff will get a judgment without you even showing up. Your response should be sent to the plaintiff and filed with the court. Any kind of response – even a letter to the judge - will result in a pre-trial conference where you can ask the judge about pro bono representation.

Three major kinds of lawsuit are associated with a Chapter 7 case:

Preferences: When filling out the Statement of Financial Affairs, you had to disclose any payments to any of your creditors of more than $600 in the last three months. If you paid back relatives, you had to disclose payments made over the last year. These payments are called "preferences" because you preferred one creditor to another. The reason for this "look-back" period prior to the Bankruptcy is that Congress didn't want you to pay all the creditors you like, while giving the ones you don't like the shaft. The look-back period is longer for "insiders," usually relatives or other individuals with power over you, because you're more likely to want to pay back a relative than a credit card company.

If you did make payments that amount to preferences, the Trustee will probably sue the recipient of that money. If you paid more than $600 to a bank in the last three months, you probably don't care. If you paid a relative, you may not be so keen on it. You will not get served with this lawsuit – it will be the relative who received the funds.

You should know that it's hard to win this kind of lawsuit. If you did make such preferential payments, your best bet is to work out a deal with the Trustee. Otherwise, the Trustee will get a judgment against your relative and will be able to garnish wages and take other steps to collect the money.

Fraudulent Conveyances: In the Statement of Financial Affairs you also had to disclose any transfers of property in the last two years. The theory behind fraudulent conveyances actually goes back to the 1500s in England, at the time of Queen Elizabeth and Shakespeare. The law does not allow you to impoverish yourself so you don't have to pay your creditors. Bankruptcy is there for people who really can't afford to pay their creditors, not for people who just don't want to.

I often have clients come into my office asking, "Should I put this car/boat/bank account/any other asset into somebody else's name?" The answer I give is always the same: No! You will be in worse shape if you try to game the system than by disclosing the property and exempting it to the extent you're able.

The time period creditors can go back to recover property you gave someone else can be as long as six years in my state, and may be even longer in other states. And if you think the Trustee won't find out about the asset because you didn't list it in the Statement of Financial Affairs, don't kid yourself. In this day of the Internet, there are no secrets.

The best defense to a fraudulent conveyance action is that you actually received "reasonably equivalent value" in exchange for the property. That value need not be money. It could be services the other person provided to you, or property the other person owns. The court generally won't argue with you about the value provided. If the Trustee says you didn't get enough for the property, as long as the value you received was "reasonable," the court typically won't quibble with your decision.

Dischargeability actions: There are two kinds of dischargeability actions: one that seeks to prevent the discharge of a specific debt, and one that seeks to prevent you from receiving a discharge at all. In general, lawsuits are filed to prevent the discharge of a specific debt when you ran up a credit card with luxury spending or took cash advances in the six month period before filing Bankruptcy. That is called the "presumption period." If you did those things, then your behavior is presumed fraudulent, and you have to prove it wasn't.

Fraud is a big no-no in the Bankruptcy Court, but it's difficult to prove.

That's because fraud is essentially a state of mind. An action taken without fraudulent intent can be legal, while the same action taken with fraudulent intent would be illegal. Courts acknowledge the fact that they can't read a person's mind, so they look to the behavior to determine if the behavior appears fraudulent.

Here's the theory behind an action to deny you the discharge of a debt: If you took large cash advances or purchased luxury goods right before filing Bankruptcy, you probably knew you couldn't pay those debts. That's why such debts are presumed to be fraudulent. Nevertheless, if you can point to other facts, you may be able to overcome that presumption and prove to the court that your actions weren't taken with fraud in mind.

Certain courts have ruled that people who used convenience checks to pay other creditors were not committing fraud, since they received no benefit from the transaction. Certain courts have ruled that a debtor who ran up gambling debts right before filing Bankruptcy were not committing fraud since, as unlikely as it may be, the debtor hoped to win money and pay the debts. Again, the court must essentially look into the mind of the debtors to determine if they had fraudulent intent when they ran up these debts.

Lawsuits to entirely deny the discharge are less common and are usually filed by the Trustee. The reasons for denying your discharge are limited, and you probably don't need to worry about them as long as you tell the truth, are honest in your dealings with the court, and cooperate with the Trustee. If you take the simple steps I detail in this book, you have nothing to worry about from this kind of lawsuit. Nevertheless, get an attorney if you're facing this kind of case. Do not fail to answer the complaint.

I need to make one final point about lawsuits in the Bankruptcy Court. If an attorney represents you in your Bankruptcy case or any other matter, just because you gave the lawsuit to the attorney doesn't mean she's representing you in that lawsuit and answering it. Make sure your attorney is answering the lawsuit. If she isn't, get another attorney or answer it yourself. Once the plaintiff has a judgment against you for failing to answer the lawsuit, it is hard to unring that bell.

Chapter 19

What Not To Do In Bankruptcy:
Bankruptcy Crimes

*T*his will be a short chapter, but an important one. People do get convicted of Bankruptcy crimes if they try to game the system. People who think they can fool the court or the officers involved in the process can go to jail.

The good news is, you won't go to jail by accident. Crime in a Bankruptcy case involves "knowingly and fraudulently" working to conceal assets; lying under oath; engaging in bribery; falsifying records; embezzling money; or trying to defraud the Bankruptcy Court. These are not things you do by accident.

As I've stated repeatedly through this book: be honest. Don't think you're smarter than everyone involved in the process. Disclose all your assets and exempt them. List all your debts. Answer the questions honestly and forthrightly. If you do those simple things, you will get the benefit that Bankruptcy is designed for: giving you relief from the debts you truly cannot afford to pay.

Chapter 20

How To Rebuild Your Credit

*B*ankruptcy will hurt your credit. That's a fact. The good news is, your credit will bounce back sooner than you think. Most of my clients are surprised how quickly their credit comes back. In fact, if you take the steps I recommend here, within one to two years you'll have reasonable credit.

A word of warning: much of this chapter is speculation. The three credit bureaus closely guard the scoring system they use to determine your credit. This chapter is based upon my observations about what seems to work, plus the observations of several industry insiders I've represented. Since the real estate market collapsed, I've had the opportunity to represent a number of people who work for banks, mortgage companies, and other lenders. They have shared their thoughts with me about what helps credit and what hurts it.

First of all, if you file Bankruptcy while your credit is still good, your credit score bounces back faster. If you wait until you have late pays and collections, your credit score takes longer to rebound. Anything on your credit report stays for up to ten years. What heals the credit report then, is time. At some point, this Bankruptcy won't even appear on your credit report. Even while it does, the further into the past it recedes, the less impact it has on your current credit score.

It appears the credit bureaus weigh recent activity more heavily than older activity. But certain activity hurts your credit score more than other kinds of activity – or does it? People assume that paying a bill late won't hurt your credit as much as a Bankruptcy. To a point, that's true. But most people don't just pay late a single time. Instead, they pay a number of their creditors late over a period of months. Say you paid three credit cards late over a period of three months. Let's say each late payment only hits your credit 20 points. Over that period, you incur a 180 point hit from those late pays. I can tell you it's rare for Bankruptcy to hit your credit score that hard.

If you wait until you have late pays and collections on your credit report and then file Bankruptcy, when your creditors look at your credit report, they'll see the late pays and collections over time, *plus* the Bankruptcy. Late pays over time seem to hit the credit rating especially hard. It appears that paying all your debts late for one month is less harmful than paying one debt late for several months. When potential lenders look at your credit report, they see all those repeated late pays in addition to the Bankruptcy. Those credit problems all add up to hurt your score.

On the other hand, if you have great credit and file Bankruptcy, when the lenders look at your credit report, they see only the Bankruptcy. That hurts you, for sure. But the problem created by the Bankruptcy isn't compounded by the repeated late pays and collections. If two people have the same financial problems and the only difference between them is one files Bankruptcy while he still has good credit, that person is in better shape than the one who decides to wait until he's desperate.

After filing Bankruptcy, what should you do? The key to rebuilding your credit, from what I've seen, is to show you can borrow a little and pay it back on time. People suggest all kinds of schemes to increase your credit score, but I believe this is the only one that works. Some of my clients say, "I never want to have a credit card again." Those clients are doomed to poor credit from now on. You need to show that you can use credit responsibly and make your payments on time.

I've been told the key is to have at least three creditors who will report your payments to the bureaus. If you have reaffirmed a debt, typically that creditor will report your payments to the bureaus. That's one creditor who will help rebuild your credit. If you have three payments you've reaffirmed, such as two car payments and a mortgage, those will count. Typically, you don't need to reaffirm a mortgage to keep the house – as long as you keep making your payments, you'll be able to keep the home. However, if you don't reaffirm, the mortgage company will not report the debt to the bureaus. Car loans and boat loans will need to be reaffirmed, and those loans get reported.

The reaffirmed debts probably won't be enough to get your credit score moving. You need to find a few more creditors to show a good payment history. A debit card with your bank won't work, even though it has the Mastercard or Visa logo on it. Using a debit card is like writing a check. You're taking the money directly out of your bank account, so you are not incurring debt and not helping your credit score.

Fortunately, there are places you can go for credit, even shortly after your Bankruptcy has been discharged. I would start with the gas stations in your area. Many of them offer credit cards even to applicants who have poor credit. The card will initially carry high interest rates and won't allow you to charge much, but you don't care. You will charge a little bit of gas every month and pay off the card every month. The finance company for the gas station will report your timely payments, which helps improve your credit score.

If you can't get a gas card, get a secured credit card. A secured credit card requires you to deposit a certain amount of money with the company, say $300 to $500, and then you can charge up to that amount on the card they issue. This is not a debit card, because they actually allow you to incur debt. They just have the deposit in case you don't make your payments. The goal here should be to charge a little every month, and pay it off every month. As you establish a good history for making your payments, the credit card company will allow you to charge more than the money you have on deposit with them, and the terms will keep getting better. Most importantly, the company will report your timely payments to the bureaus, and each month that passes with timely payments will improve your credit score. To find a secured credit card issuer, simply Google "secured credit card" and the issuers will show up.

From everything I've seen and read, if you have twelve months of solid payments, your credit will be in decent shape. As time goes by and the Bankruptcy fades into the past, your credit will continue to improve. The biggest myth out there is that your credit doesn't bounce back. You'll be surprised how quickly it does.

Chapter 21

Can I Do This On My Own?

I won't lie to you. You'll need a strong stomach to do a Chapter 7 Bankruptcy on your own. It can be done, however, and many people have successfully completed the process. If you're up for it, have a relatively straight-forward case, and are willing to follow the guidance in this book, you can manage fine on your own.

You do have one other option. The Bankruptcy Code provides for the possibility of non-attorney petition preparers who help people complete the Bankruptcy petition. Since the preparer isn't an attorney, that person cannot offer legal advice. Nevertheless, he can help you make sure you put the right number in the right place, making the process less intimidating. Obviously, a person offering this limited service would charge less than an attorney's fee.

My website *myeasy7.com* will walk you through the process of completing the petition. The information is valid in all fifty states and will save you time and frustration. I recommend this option if you need help completing the paperwork.

This book is designed to help you file Chapter 7 Bankruptcy on your own, with no assistance other than an Internet connection. If you're up for it, you can succeed. Combining the book with the assistance of a Bankruptcy petition preparer or a website such as *myeasy7.com* is a less challenging approach, and still affordable. At a minimum, this book can help you ask an attorney the right questions, should you decide to hire one. Whichever route you choose, if you're in debt and have no way to pay your bill, Bankruptcy may be the best solution for you.

Appendix A

Sample Forms and Filings

B 1 (Official Form 1) (1/08)

United States Bankruptcy Court Southern District of California	

Name of Debtor (if individual, enter Last, First, Middle): **Sample, Joseph Allan Jr.**	Name of Joint Debtor (Spouse) (Last, First, Middle): **Sample, Jane Ann**
All Other Names used by the Debtor in the last 8 years (include married, maiden, and trade names): **FDBA The Sample Company**	All Other Names used by the Joint Debtor in the last 8 years (include married, maiden, and trade names): **FKA Jane Ann Maiden**
Last four digits of Soc. Sec. or Individual-Taxpayer I.D. (ITIN) No./Complete EIN (if more than one, state all): **6789**	Last four digits of Soc. Sec. or Individual-Taxpayer I.D. (ITIN) No./Complete EIN (if more than one, state all): **5678**
Street Address of Debtor (No. and Street, City, and State): **123 Avenue** **Beverly Hills, CA** ZIP CODE **90210**	Street Address of Joint Debtor (No. and Street, City, and State): **123 Avenue** **Beverly Hills, CA** ZIP CODE **90210**
County of Residence or of the Principal Place of Business: **Los Angeles**	County of Residence or of the Principal Place of Business: **Los Angeles**
Mailing Address of Debtor (if different from street address): **PO Box 123** **Beverly Hills, CA** ZIP CODE **90210**	Mailing Address of Joint Debtor (if different from street address): **PO Box 123** **Beverly Hills, CA** ZIP CODE **90210**
Location of Principal Assets of Business Debtor (if different from street address above): ZIP CODE	

Type of Debtor (Form of Organization) (Check one box.)	Nature of Business (Check one box.)	Chapter of Bankruptcy Code Under Which the Petition is Filed (Check one box.)
☑ Individual (includes Joint Debtors) *See Exhibit D on page 2 of this form.* ☐ Corporation (includes LLC and LLP) ☐ Partnership ☐ Other (If debtor is not one of the above entities, check this box and state type of entity below.)	☐ Health Care Business ☐ Single Asset Real Estate as defined in 11 U.S.C. § 101(51B) ☐ Railroad ☐ Stockbroker ☐ Commodity Broker ☐ Clearing Bank ☐ Other	☑ Chapter 7 ☐ Chapter 15 Petition for ☐ Chapter 9 Recognition of a Foreign ☐ Chapter 11 Main Proceeding ☐ Chapter 12 ☐ Chapter 15 Petition for ☐ Chapter 13 Recognition of a Foreign Nonmain Proceeding
	Tax-Exempt Entity (Check box, if applicable.) ☐ Debtor is a tax-exempt organization under Title 26 of the United States Code (the Internal Revenue Code).	**Nature of Debts** (Check one box.) ☑ Debts are primarily consumer debts, defined in 11 U.S.C. § 101(8) as "incurred by an individual primarily for a personal, family, or household purpose." ☐ Debts are primarily business debts.

Filing Fee (Check one box.)	Chapter 11 Debtors
☑ Full Filing Fee attached. ☐ Filing Fee to be paid in installments (applicable to individuals only). Must attach signed application for the court's consideration certifying that the debtor is unable to pay fee except in installments. Rule 1006(b). See Official Form 3A. ☐ Filing Fee waiver requested (applicable to chapter 7 individuals only). Must attach signed application for the court's consideration. See Official Form 3B.	Check one box: ☐ Debtor is a small business debtor as defined in 11 U.S.C. § 101(51D). ☐ Debtor is not a small business debtor as defined in 11 U.S.C. § 101(51D). Check if: ☐ Debtor's aggregate noncontingent liquidated debts (excluding debts owed to insiders or affiliates) are less than $2,190,000. - Check all applicable boxes: ☐ A plan is being filed with this petition. ☐ Acceptances of the plan were solicited prepetition from one or more classes of creditors, in accordance with 11 U.S.C. § 1126(b).

Statistical/Administrative Information	THIS SPACE IS FOR COURT USE ONLY
☐ Debtor estimates that funds will be available for distribution to unsecured creditors. ☑ Debtor estimates that, after any exempt property is excluded and administrative expenses paid, there will be no funds available for distribution to unsecured creditors.	

Estimated Number of Creditors

☑ 1-49	☐ 50-99	☐ 100-199	☐ 200-999	☐ 1,000-5,000	☐ 5,001-10,000	☐ 10,001-25,000	☐ 25,001-50,000	☐ 50,001-100,000	☐ Over 100,000

Estimated Assets

☐ $0 to $50,000	☐ $50,001 to $100,000	☑ $100,001 to $500,000	☐ $500,001 to $1 million	☐ $1,000,001 to $10 million	☐ $10,000,001 to $50 million	☐ $50,000,001 to $100 million	☐ $100,000,001 to $500 million	☐ $500,000,001 to $1 billion	☐ More than $1 billion

Estimated Liabilities

☐ $0 to $50,000	☐ $50,001 to $100,000	☑ $100,001 to $500,000	☐ $500,001 to $1 million	☐ $1,000,001 to $10 million	☐ $10,000,001 to $50 million	☐ $50,000,001 to $100 million	☐ $100,000,001 to $500 million	☐ $500,000,001 to $1 billion	☐ More than $1 billion

B 1 (Official Form 1) (1/08)   Page 2

Voluntary Petition *(This page must be completed and filed in every case.)*	Name of Debtor(s): Sample, Joseph Allan Jr. and Sample, Jane Ann

All Prior Bankruptcy Cases Filed Within Last 8 Years (If more than two, attach additional sheet.)

Location Where Filed:	Case Number:	Date Filed:
Location Where Filed:	Case Number:	Date Filed:

Pending Bankruptcy Case Filed by any Spouse, Partner, or Affiliate of this Debtor (If more than one, attach additional sheet.)

Name of Debtor:	Case Number:	Date Filed:
District: **Southern District of California**	Relationship:	Judge:

Exhibit A	Exhibit B
(To be completed if debtor is required to file periodic reports (e.g., forms 10K and 10Q) with the Securities and Exchange Commission pursuant to Section 13 or 15(d) of the Securities Exchange Act of 1934 and is requesting relief under chapter 11.)	(To be completed if debtor is an individual whose debts are primarily consumer debts.) I, the attorney for the petitioner named in the foregoing petition, declare that I have informed the petitioner that [he or she] may proceed under chapter 7, 11, 12, or 13 of title 11, United States Code, and have explained the relief available under each such chapter. I further certify that I have delivered to the debtor the notice required by 11 U.S.C. § 342(b).
☐ Exhibit A is attached and made a part of this petition.	X _____ Signature of Attorney for Debtor(s) (Date)

Exhibit C

Does the debtor own or have possession of any property that poses or is alleged to pose a threat of imminent and identifiable harm to public health or safety?

☐ Yes, and Exhibit C is attached and made a part of this petition.

☑ No.

Exhibit D

(To be completed by every individual debtor. If a joint petition is filed, each spouse must complete and attach a separate Exhibit D.)

☑ Exhibit D completed and signed by the debtor is attached and made a part of this petition.

If this is a joint petition:

☑ Exhibit D also completed and signed by the joint debtor is attached and made a part of this petition.

Information Regarding the Debtor - Venue
(Check any applicable box.)

☑ Debtor has been domiciled or has had a residence, principal place of business, or principal assets in this District for 180 days immediately preceding the date of this petition or for a longer part of such 180 days than in any other District.

☐ There is a bankruptcy case concerning debtor's affiliate, general partner, or partnership pending in this District.

☐ Debtor is a debtor in a foreign proceeding and has its principal place of business or principal assets in the United States in this District, or has no principal place of business or assets in the United States but is a defendant in an action or proceeding [in a federal or state court] in this District, or the interests of the parties will be served in regard to the relief sought in this District.

Certification by a Debtor Who Resides as a Tenant of Residential Property
(Check all applicable boxes.)

☐ Landlord has a judgment against the debtor for possession of debtor's residence. (If box checked, complete the following.)

_____
(Name of landlord that obtained judgment)

_____
(Address of landlord)

☐ Debtor claims that under applicable nonbankruptcy law, there are circumstances under which the debtor would be permitted to cure the entire monetary default that gave rise to the judgment for possession, after the judgment for possession was entered, and

☐ Debtor has included with this petition the deposit with the court of any rent that would become due during the 30-day period after the filing of the petition.

☐ Debtor certifies that he/she has served the Landlord with this certification. (11 U.S.C. § 362(l)).

B 1 (Official Form) 1 (1/08)	Page 3
Voluntary Petition *(This page must be completed and filed in every case.)*	Name of Debtor(s): **Sample, Joseph Allan Jr. and Sample, Jane Ann**

Signatures

Signature(s) of Debtor(s) (Individual/Joint)	**Signature of a Foreign Representative**

I declare under penalty of perjury that the information provided in this petition is true and correct.
 [If petitioner is an individual whose debts are primarily consumer debts and has chosen to file under chapter 7] I am aware that I may proceed under chapter 7, 11, 12 or 13 of title 11, United States Code, understand the relief available under each such chapter, and choose to proceed under chapter 7.
 [If no attorney represents me and no bankruptcy petition preparer signs the petition] I have obtained and read the notice required by 11 U.S.C. § 342(b).
 	
 I request relief in accordance with the chapter of title 11, United States Code, specified in this petition.
 	
 X _____
    Signature of Debtor
 	
 X _____
    Signature of Joint Debtor
 	
    Telephone Number (if not represented by attorney)
 	
    Date
	I declare under penalty of perjury that the information provided in this petition is true and correct, that I am the foreign representative of a debtor in a foreign proceeding, and that I am authorized to file this petition.
	
	 (Check only one box.)
	
	 ☐ I request relief in accordance with chapter 15 of title 11, United States Code. Certified copies of the documents required by 11 U.S.C. § 1515 are attached.
	
	 ☐ Pursuant to 11 U.S.C. § 1511, I request relief in accordance with the chapter of title 11 specified in this petition. A certified copy of the order granting recognition of the foreign main proceeding is attached.
	
	 X _____
	    (Signature of Foreign Representative)
	
	    (Printed Name of Foreign Representative)
	
	    Date

Signature of Attorney*
 	
 X _____
    Signature of Attorney for Debtor(s)
 	
    Printed Name of Attorney for Debtor(s)
 	
    Firm Name
 	
    Address
 	
    Telephone Number
 	
    Date
 	
 *In a case in which § 707(b)(4)(D) applies, this signature also constitutes a certification that the attorney has no knowledge after an inquiry that the information in the schedules is incorrect.
	Signature of Non-Attorney Bankruptcy Petition Preparer
	
	 I declare under penalty of perjury that: (1) I am a bankruptcy petition preparer as defined in 11 U.S.C. § 110; (2) I prepared this document for compensation and have provided the debtor with a copy of this document and the notices and information required under 11 U.S.C. §§ 110(b), 110(h), and 342(b); and, (3) if rules or guidelines have been promulgated pursuant to 11 U.S.C. § 110(h) setting a maximum fee for services chargeable by bankruptcy petition preparers, I have given the debtor notice of the maximum amount before preparing any document for filing for a debtor or accepting any fee from the debtor, as required in that section. Official Form 19 is attached.
	
	    Printed Name and title, if any, of Bankruptcy Petition Preparer
	
	    Social-Security number (If the bankruptcy petition preparer is not an individual, state the Social-Security number of the officer, principal, responsible person or partner of the bankruptcy petition preparer.) (Required by 11 U.S.C. § 110.)
	
	    Address
	
	 X _____
	
	    Date
	
	 Signature of bankruptcy petition preparer or officer, principal, responsible person, or partner whose Social-Security number is provided above.

Signature of Debtor (Corporation/Partnership)
 	
 I declare under penalty of perjury that the information provided in this petition is true and correct, and that I have been authorized to file this petition on behalf of the debtor.
 	
 The debtor requests the relief in accordance with the chapter of title 11, United States Code, specified in this petition.
 	
 X _____
    Signature of Authorized Individual
 	
    Printed Name of Authorized Individual
 	
    Title of Authorized Individual
 	
    Date
	Names and Social-Security numbers of all other individuals who prepared or assisted in preparing this document unless the bankruptcy petition preparer is not an individual.
	
	 If more than one person prepared this document, attach additional sheets conforming to the appropriate official form for each person.
	
	 A bankruptcy petition preparer's failure to comply with the provisions of title 11 and the Federal Rules of Bankruptcy Procedure may result in fines or imprisonment or both. 11 U.S.C. § 110; 18 U.S.C. § 156.

B 1D (Official Form 1, Exhibit D) (12/09)

UNITED STATES BANKRUPTCY COURT

Southern District of California

In re Joseph Allan Sample, Jr; Jane   Case No._____
Debtor   (if known)

EXHIBIT D - INDIVIDUAL DEBTOR'S STATEMENT OF COMPLIANCE WITH CREDIT COUNSELING REQUIREMENT

Warning: You must be able to check truthfully one of the five statements regarding credit counseling listed below. If you cannot do so, you are not eligible to file a bankruptcy case, and the court can dismiss any case you do file. If that happens, you will lose whatever filing fee you paid, and your creditors will be able to resume collection activities against you. If your case is dismissed and you file another bankruptcy case later, you may be required to pay a second filing fee and you may have to take extra steps to stop creditors' collection activities.

Every individual debtor must file this Exhibit D. If a joint petition is filed, each spouse must complete and file a separate Exhibit D. Check one of the five statements below and attach any documents as directed.

☑ 1. Within the 180 days **before the filing of my bankruptcy case,** I received a briefing from a credit counseling agency approved by the United States trustee or bankruptcy administrator that outlined the opportunities for available credit counseling and assisted me in performing a related budget analysis, and I have a certificate from the agency describing the services provided to me. *Attach a copy of the certificate and a copy of any debt repayment plan developed through the agency.*

☐ 2. Within the 180 days **before the filing of my bankruptcy case,** I received a briefing from a credit counseling agency approved by the United States trustee or bankruptcy administrator that outlined the opportunities for available credit counseling and assisted me in performing a related budget analysis, but I do not have a certificate from the agency describing the services provided to me. *You must file a copy of a certificate from the agency describing the services provided to you and a copy of any debt repayment plan developed through the agency no later than 14 days after your bankruptcy case is filed.*

B 1D (Official Form 1, Exh. D) (12/09) – Cont.

❒ 3. I certify that I requested credit counseling services from an approved agency but was unable to obtain the services during the seven days from the time I made my request, and the following exigent circumstances merit a temporary waiver of the credit counseling requirement so I can file my bankruptcy case now. *[Summarize exigent circumstances here.]*

If your certification is satisfactory to the court, you must still obtain the credit counseling briefing within the first 30 days after you file your bankruptcy petition and promptly file a certificate from the agency that provided the counseling, together with a copy of any debt management plan developed through the agency. Failure to fulfill these requirements may result in dismissal of your case. Any extension of the 30-day deadline can be granted only for cause and is limited to a maximum of 15 days. Your case may also be dismissed if the court is not satisfied with your reasons for filing your bankruptcy case without first receiving a credit counseling briefing.

❒ 4. I am not required to receive a credit counseling briefing because of: *[Check the applicable statement.] [Must be accompanied by a motion for determination by the court.]*

❒ Incapacity. (Defined in 11 U.S.C. § 109(h)(4) as impaired by reason of mental illness or mental deficiency so as to be incapable of realizing and making rational decisions with respect to financial responsibilities.);
❒ Disability. (Defined in 11 U.S.C. § 109(h)(4) as physically impaired to the extent of being unable, after reasonable effort, to participate in a credit counseling briefing in person, by telephone, or through the Internet.);
❒ Active military duty in a military combat zone.

❒ 5. The United States trustee or bankruptcy administrator has determined that the credit counseling requirement of 11 U.S.C. § 109(h) does not apply in this district.

I certify under penalty of perjury that the information provided above is true and correct.

Signature of Debtor: _____

Date: _____

B 1D (Official Form 1, Exhibit D) (12/09)

UNITED STATES BANKRUPTCY COURT

Southern District of California

In re Joseph Allan Sample, Jr; Jane   Case No. _____
           Debtor   (if known)

EXHIBIT D - INDIVIDUAL DEBTOR'S STATEMENT OF COMPLIANCE WITH CREDIT COUNSELING REQUIREMENT

Warning: You must be able to check truthfully one of the five statements regarding credit counseling listed below. If you cannot do so, you are not eligible to file a bankruptcy case, and the court can dismiss any case you do file. If that happens, you will lose whatever filing fee you paid, and your creditors will be able to resume collection activities against you. If your case is dismissed and you file another bankruptcy case later, you may be required to pay a second filing fee and you may have to take extra steps to stop creditors' collection activities.

Every individual debtor must file this Exhibit D. If a joint petition is filed, each spouse must complete and file a separate Exhibit D. Check one of the five statements below and attach any documents as directed.

☒ 1. Within the 180 days **before the filing of my bankruptcy case,** I received a briefing from a credit counseling agency approved by the United States trustee or bankruptcy administrator that outlined the opportunities for available credit counseling and assisted me in performing a related budget analysis, and I have a certificate from the agency describing the services provided to me. *Attach a copy of the certificate and a copy of any debt repayment plan developed through the agency.*

☐ 2. Within the 180 days **before the filing of my bankruptcy case,** I received a briefing from a credit counseling agency approved by the United States trustee or bankruptcy administrator that outlined the opportunities for available credit counseling and assisted me in performing a related budget analysis, but I do not have a certificate from the agency describing the services provided to me. *You must file a copy of a certificate from the agency describing the services provided to you and a copy of any debt repayment plan developed through the agency no later than 14 days after your bankruptcy case is filed.*

B 1D (Official Form 1, Exh. D) (12/09) – Cont.   Page 2

☐ 3. I certify that I requested credit counseling services from an approved agency but was unable to obtain the services during the seven days from the time I made my request, and the following exigent circumstances merit a temporary waiver of the credit counseling requirement so I can file my bankruptcy case now. *[Summarize exigent circumstances here.]*

If your certification is satisfactory to the court, you must still obtain the credit counseling briefing within the first 30 days after you file your bankruptcy petition and promptly file a certificate from the agency that provided the counseling, together with a copy of any debt management plan developed through the agency. Failure to fulfill these requirements may result in dismissal of your case. Any extension of the 30-day deadline can be granted only for cause and is limited to a maximum of 15 days. Your case may also be dismissed if the court is not satisfied with your reasons for filing your bankruptcy case without first receiving a credit counseling briefing.

☐ 4. I am not required to receive a credit counseling briefing because of: *[Check the applicable statement.] [Must be accompanied by a motion for determination by the court.]*

☐ Incapacity. (Defined in 11 U.S.C. § 109(h)(4) as impaired by reason of mental illness or mental deficiency so as to be incapable of realizing and making rational decisions with respect to financial responsibilities.);
☐ Disability. (Defined in 11 U.S.C. § 109(h)(4) as physically impaired to the extent of being unable, after reasonable effort, to participate in a credit counseling briefing in person, by telephone, or through the Internet.);
☐ Active military duty in a military combat zone.

☐ 5. The United States trustee or bankruptcy administrator has determined that the credit counseling requirement of 11 U.S.C. § 109(h) does not apply in this district.

I certify under penalty of perjury that the information provided above is true and correct.

Signature of Debtor: _____

Date: _____

136

Michael Greiner, J.D

B6 Summary (Official Form 6 - Summary) (12/07)

United States Bankruptcy Court

Southern District of California

In re Joseph Allan Sample, Jr; Jane Ann S ,
        Debtor

Case No. _____

Chapter 7 _____

SUMMARY OF SCHEDULES

Indicate as to each schedule whether that schedule is attached and state the number of pages in each. Report the totals from Schedules A, B, D, E, F, I, and J in the boxes provided. Add the amounts from Schedules A and B to determine the total amount of the debtor's assets. Add the amounts of all claims from Schedules D, E, and F to determine the total amount of the debtor's liabilities. Individual debtors also must complete the "Statistical Summary of Certain Liabilities and Related Data" if they file a case under chapter 7, 11, or 13.

NAME OF SCHEDULE	ATTACHED (YES/NO)	NO. OF SHEETS	ASSETS	LIABILITIES	OTHER
A - Real Property	Yes	1	$ 100,000.00		
B - Personal Property	Yes	3	$ 33,525.00		
C - Property Claimed as Exempt	Yes	1			
D - Creditors Holding Secured Claims	Yes	1		$ 101,000.00	
E - Creditors Holding Unsecured Priority Claims (Total of Claims on Schedule E)	Yes	4		$ 1,000.00	
F - Creditors Holding Unsecured Nonpriority Claims	Yes	1		$ 30,000.00	
G - Executory Contracts and Unexpired Leases	Yes	1			
H - Codebtors	Yes	1			
I - Current Income of Individual Debtor(s)	Yes	1			$ 3,300.00
J - Current Expenditures of Individual Debtors(s)	Yes	2			$ 3,300.00
TOTAL		16	$ 133,525.00	$ 132,000.00	

B 6 Summary (Official Form 6 - Summary) (12/07)

United States Bankruptcy Court

Southern District of California

In re Joseph Allan Sample, Jr; Jane Ann S ,
        Debtor

Case No. _____

Chapter _7_____

STATISTICAL SUMMARY OF CERTAIN LIABILITIES AND RELATED DATA (28 U.S.C. § 159)

If you are an individual debtor whose debts are primarily consumer debts, as defined in § 101(8) of the Bankruptcy Code (11 U.S.C. § 101(8)), filing a case under chapter 7, 11 or 13, you must report all information requested below.

☐ Check this box if you are an individual debtor whose debts are NOT primarily consumer debts. You are not required to report any information here.

This information is for statistical purposes only under 28 U.S.C. § 159.

Summarize the following types of liabilities, as reported in the Schedules, and total them.

Type of Liability	Amount
Domestic Support Obligations (from Schedule E)	$ 0.00
Taxes and Certain Other Debts Owed to Governmental Units (from Schedule E)	$ 1,000.00
Claims for Death or Personal Injury While Debtor Was Intoxicated (from Schedule E) (whether disputed or undisputed)	$ 0.00
Student Loan Obligations (from Schedule F)	$ 0.00
Domestic Support, Separation Agreement, and Divorce Decree Obligations Not Reported on Schedule E	$ 0.00
Obligations to Pension or Profit-Sharing, and Other Similar Obligations (from Schedule F)	$ 0.00
TOTAL	$ 1,000.00

State the following:

Average Income (from Schedule I, Line 16)	$ 3,300.00
Average Expenses (from Schedule J, Line 18)	$ 3,300.00
Current Monthly Income (from Form 22A Line 12; OR, Form 22B Line 11; OR, Form 22C Line 20)	$ 4,000.00

State the following:

1. Total from Schedule D, "UNSECURED PORTION, IF ANY" column		$ 0.00
2. Total from Schedule E, "AMOUNT ENTITLED TO PRIORITY" column.	$ 1,000.00	
3. Total from Schedule E, "AMOUNT NOT ENTITLED TO PRIORITY, IF ANY" column		$ 0.00
4. Total from Schedule F		$ 30,000.00
5. Total of non-priority unsecured debt (sum of 1, 3, and 4)		$ 30,000.00

B6A (Official Form 6A) (12/07)

In re Joseph Allan Sample, Jr; Jane Ann Sampl____,   Case No. _____
                    Debtor   (If known)

SCHEDULE A - REAL PROPERTY

Except as directed below, list all real property in which the debtor has any legal, equitable, or future interest, including all property owned as a co-tenant, community property, or in which the debtor has a life estate. Include any property in which the debtor holds rights and powers exercisable for the debtor's own benefit. If the debtor is married, state whether the husband, wife, both, or the marital community own the property by placing an "H," "W," "J," or "C" in the column labeled "Husband, Wife, Joint, or Community." If the debtor holds no interest in real property, write "None" under "Description and Location of Property."

Do not include interests in executory contracts and unexpired leases on this schedule. List them in Schedule G - Executory Contracts and Unexpired Leases.

If an entity claims to have a lien or hold a secured interest in any property, state the amount of the secured claim. See Schedule D. If no entity claims to hold a secured interest in the property, write "None" in the column labeled "Amount of Secured Claim."

If the debtor is an individual or if a joint petition is filed, state the amount of any exemption claimed in the property only in Schedule C - Property Claimed as Exempt.

DESCRIPTION AND LOCATION OF PROPERTY	NATURE OF DEBTOR'S INTEREST IN PROPERTY	HUSBAND, WIFE, JOINT, OR COMMUNITY	CURRENT VALUE OF DEBTOR'S INTEREST IN PROPERTY, WITHOUT DEDUCTING ANY SECURED CLAIM OR EXEMPTION	AMOUNT OF SECURED CLAIM
Debtors' homestead Location: 123 Avenue, Beverly Hil	Fee simple	J	100,000.00	95000
			Total▶ 100,000.00	

(Report also on Summary of Schedules.)

B 6B (Official Form 6B) (12/07)

In re Sample, Joseph Allan Jr. and Sample, Jane A ,   Case No. _____
            Debtor   (If known)

SCHEDULE B - PERSONAL PROPERTY

Except as directed below, list all personal property of the debtor of whatever kind. If the debtor has no property in one or more of the categories, place an "x" in the appropriate position in the column labeled "None." If additional space is needed in any category, attach a separate sheet properly identified with the case name, case number, and the number of the category. If the debtor is married, state whether the husband, wife, both, or the marital community own the property by placing an "H," "W," "J," or "C" in the column labeled "Husband, Wife, Joint, or Community." If the debtor is an individual or a joint petition is filed, state the amount of any exemptions claimed only in Schedule C - Property Claimed as Exempt.

Do not list interests in executory contracts and unexpired leases on this schedule. List them in Schedule G - Executory Contracts and Unexpired Leases.

If the property is being held for the debtor by someone else, state that person's name and address under "Description and Location of Property." If the property is being held for a minor child, simply state the child's initials and the name and address of the child's parent or guardian, such as "A.B., a minor child, by John Doe, guardian." Do not disclose the child's name. See, 11 U.S.C. §112 and Fed. R. Bankr. P. 1007(m).

TYPE OF PROPERTY	N O N E	DESCRIPTION AND LOCATION OF PROPERTY	HUSBAND, WIFE, JOINT, OR COMMUNITY	CURRENT VALUE OF DEBTOR'S INTEREST IN PROPERTY, WITHOUT DEDUCTING ANY SECURED CLAIM OR EXEMPTION
1. Cash on hand.				
2. Checking, savings or other financial accounts, certificates of deposit or shares in banks, savings and loan, thrift, building and loan, and homestead associations, or credit unions, brokerage houses, or cooperatives.		checking account Location: Bank of America	J	400.00
3. Security deposits with public utilities, telephone companies, landlords, and others.				
4. Household goods and furnishings, including audio, video, and computer equipment.		miscellaneous household goods and furnishings Location: 123 Avenue, Beverly Hills, CA	J	2,000.00
5. Books; pictures and other art objects; antiques; stamp, coin, record, tape, compact disc, and other collections or collectibles.				
6. Wearing apparel.		miscellaneous wearing apparel	J	500.00
7. Furs and jewelry.		miscellaneous jewelry	W	2,000.00
8. Firearms and sports, photographic, and other hobby equipment.				
9. Interests in insurance policies. Name insurance company of each policy and itemize surrender or refund value of each.		cash value life insurance policy Location: Primerica	H	2,500.00
10. Annuities. Itemize and name each issuer.				
11. Interests in an education IRA as defined in 26 U.S.C. § 530(b)(1) or under a qualified State tuition plan as defined in 26 U.S.C. § 529(b)(1). Give particulars. (File separately the record(s) of any such interest(s). 11 U.S.C. § 521(c).)				

B 6B (Official Form 6B) (12/07) -- Cont.

In re Sample, Joseph Allan Jr. and Sample, Jane A　　　　　　Case No. _____
　　　　　　　　　Debtor　　　　　　　　　　　　　　　　　　　　　　　　　(If known)

SCHEDULE B - PERSONAL PROPERTY
(Continuation Sheet)

TYPE OF PROPERTY	N O N E	DESCRIPTION AND LOCATION OF PROPERTY	HUSBAND, WIFE, JOINT, OR COMMUNITY	CURRENT VALUE OF DEBTOR'S INTEREST IN PROPERTY, WITH-OUT DEDUCTING ANY SECURED CLAIM OR EXEMPTION
12. Interests in IRA, ERISA, Keogh, or other pension or profit sharing plans. Give particulars.		401K Location: Fidelity	W	10,000.00
13. Stock and interests in incorporated and unincorporated businesses. Itemize.		Sample Business Inc, only assets are bank account (Chase, $1000), tools and equipment ($500)	H	1,500.00
14. Interests in partnerships or joint ventures. Itemize.				
15. Government and corporate bonds and other negotiable and non-negotiable instruments.				
16. Accounts receivable.				
17. Alimony, maintenance, support, and property settlements to which the debtor is or may be entitled. Give particulars.				
18. Other liquidated debts owed to debtor including tax refunds. Give particulars.		anticipated 2010 tax refund prorated Location: IRS and State Department of Treasury	J	2,000.00
19. Equitable or future interests, life estates, and rights or powers exercisable for the benefit of the debtor other than those listed in Schedule A – Real Property.				
20. Contingent and noncontingent interests in estate of a decedent, death benefit plan, life insurance policy, or trust.				
21. Other contingent and unliquidated claims of every nature, including tax refunds, counterclaims of the debtor, and rights to setoff claims. Give estimated value of each.				

B 6B (Official Form 6B) (12/07) -- Cont.

In re <u>Sample, Joseph Allan Jr. and Sample, Jane A</u> ,   Case No. _____
          Debtor   (If known)

SCHEDULE B - PERSONAL PROPERTY
(Continuation Sheet)

TYPE OF PROPERTY	N O N E	DESCRIPTION AND LOCATION OF PROPERTY	HUSBAND, WIFE, JOINT, OR COMMUNITY	CURRENT VALUE OF DEBTOR'S INTEREST IN PROPERTY, WITH-OUT DEDUCTING ANY SECURED CLAIM OR EXEMPTION
22. Patents, copyrights, and other intellectual property. Give particulars.				
23. Licenses, franchises, and other general intangibles. Give particulars.				
24. Customer lists or other compilations containing personally identifiable information (as defined in 11 U.S.C. § 101(41A)) provided to the debtor by individuals in connection with obtaining a product or service from the debtor primarily for personal, family, or household purposes.				
25. Automobiles, trucks, trailers, and other vehicles and accessories.		2006 Toyota Rav4, 60,000 miles Location: 123 Avenue, Beverly Hills CA	J	12,625.00
26. Boats, motors, and accessories.				
27. Aircraft and accessories.				
28. Office equipment, furnishings, and supplies.				
29. Machinery, fixtures, equipment, and supplies used in business.				
30. Inventory.				
31. Animals.				
32. Crops - growing or harvested. Give particulars.				
33. Farming equipment and implements.				
34. Farm supplies, chemicals, and feed.				
35. Other personal property of any kind not already listed. Itemize.				

_____0_____ continuation sheets attached   Total▶ $ 13,500.00

(Include amounts from any continuation sheets attached. Report total also on Summary of Schedules.)

B 6C (Official Form 6C) (12/07)

In re Sample, Joseph Allan Jr. and Sample, Jan ,   Case No. _____
                Debtor   (If known)

SCHEDULE C - PROPERTY CLAIMED AS EXEMPT

Debtor claims the exemptions to which debtor is entitled under: ☐ Check if debtor claims a homestead exemption that exceeds
(Check one box) $136,875.
☑ 11 U.S.C. § 522(b)(2)
☐ 11 U.S.C. § 522(b)(3)

DESCRIPTION OF PROPERTY	SPECIFY LAW PROVIDING EACH EXEMPTION	VALUE OF CLAIMED EXEMPTION	CURRENT VALUE OF PROPERTY WITHOUT DEDUCTING EXEMPTION
checking account	11 USC sec 522(d)(5)	400.00	400.00
household goods and furnishings	11 USC sec 522(d)(3)	2,000.00	2,000.00
wearing apparel	11 USC sec 522(d)(3)	500.00	500.00
jewelry	11 USC sec 522(d)(4) 11 USC sec 522(d)(5)	2,000.00	2,000.00
cash value life insurance policy	11 USC sec 522(d)(5)	2,500.00	2,500.00
Sample Business Inc.	11 USC sec 522(d)(5)	1,500.00	1,500.00
401K	11 USC sec 522(d)(12)	10,000.00	10,000.00
anticipated 2010 tax refund prorated	11 USC sec 522(d)(5)	2,000.00	2,000.00
2006 Toyota Rav4	11 USC sec 522(d)(2) 11 USC sec 522(d)(5)	6,625.00	12,625.00
Debtors homestead	11 USC sec 522(d)(1)	5,000.00	100,000.00

B 6D (Official Form 6D) (12/07)

In re Sample, Joseph Allan Jr. and Sample, ,   Case No. _____
_____ Debtor   (If known)

SCHEDULE D - CREDITORS HOLDING SECURED CLAIMS

State the name, mailing address, including zip code, and last four digits of any account number of all entities holding claims secured by property of the debtor as of the date of filing of the petition. The complete account number of any account the debtor has with the creditor is useful to the trustee and the creditor and may be provided if the debtor chooses to do so. List creditors holding all types of secured interests such as judgment liens, garnishments, statutory liens, mortgages, deeds of trust, and other security interests.

List creditors in alphabetical order to the extent practicable. If a minor child is the creditor, state the child's initials and the name and address of the child's parent or guardian, such as "A.B., a minor child, by John Doe, guardian." Do not disclose the child's name. See, 11 U.S.C. §112 and Fed. R. Bankr. P. 1007(m). If all secured creditors will not fit on this page, use the continuation sheet provided.

If any entity other than a spouse in a joint case may be jointly liable on a claim, place an "X" in the column labeled "Codebtor," include the entity on the appropriate schedule of creditors, and complete Schedule H – Codebtors. If a joint petition is filed, state whether the husband, wife, both of them, or the marital community may be liable on each claim by placing an "H," "W," "J," or "C" in the column labeled "Husband, Wife, Joint, or Community."

If the claim is contingent, place an "X" in the column labeled "Contingent." If the claim is unliquidated, place an "X" in the column labeled "Unliquidated." If the claim is disputed, place an "X" in the column labeled "Disputed." (You may need to place an "X" in more than one of these three columns.)

Total the columns labeled "Amount of Claim Without Deducting Value of Collateral" and "Unsecured Portion, if Any" in the boxes labeled "Total(s)" on the last sheet of the completed schedule. Report the total from the column labeled "Amount of Claim Without Deducting Value of Collateral" also on the Summary of Schedules and, if the debtor is an individual with primarily consumer debts, report the total from the column labeled "Unsecured Portion, if Any" on the Statistical Summary of Certain Liabilities and Related Data.

☐   Check this box if debtor has no creditors holding secured claims to report on this Schedule D.

CREDITOR'S NAME AND MAILING ADDRESS INCLUDING ZIP CODE AND AN ACCOUNT NUMBER *(See Instructions Above.)*	CODEBTOR	HUSBAND, WIFE, JOINT, OR COMMUNITY	DATE CLAIM WAS INCURRED, NATURE OF LIEN , AND DESCRIPTION AND VALUE OF PROPERTY SUBJECT TO LIEN	CONTINGENT	UNLIQUIDATED	DISPUTED	AMOUNT OF CLAIM WITHOUT DEDUCTING VALUE OF COLLATERAL	UNSECURED PORTION, IF ANY
ACCOUNT NO.1234 Bank of America PO Box 15184 Wilmington, DE 19850-5184	X	J	2006 2nd mortgage Debtors' homestead VALUE $ 100,000.00				15,000.00	0.00
ACCOUNT NO.1234 CitiMortgage 1000 Technology Drive O'Fallon, MO 63368		J	2006 First Mortgage Debtors' homestead VALUE $ 100,000.00				80,000.00	0.00
ACCOUNT NO.1234 Toyota Motor Credit Co. 5005 North River Blvd., NE Cedar Rapids, IA 52411-6634		J	2006 Purchase Money Security 2006 Toyota Rav VALUE $ 12,625.00				6,000.00	0.00
0 continuation sheets attached			Subtotal ▶ (Total of this page)				$ 101,000.00	$ 0.00
			Total ▶ (Use only on last page)				$ 101,000.00	$ 0.00
							(Report also on Summary of Schedules.)	(If applicable, report also on Statistical Summary of Certain Liabilities and Related Data.)

Michael Greiner, J.D

B 6D (Official Form 6D) (12/07) – Cont.

In re Sample, Joseph Allan Jr. and Sample, ,
        Debtor

Case No. _____
                    (if known)

SCHEDULE D - CREDITORS HOLDING SECURED CLAIMS
(Continuation Sheet)

CREDITOR'S NAME AND MAILING ADDRESS INCLUDING ZIP CODE AND AN ACCOUNT NUMBER (See Instructions Above.)	CODEBTOR	HUSBAND, WIFE, JOINT, OR COMMUNITY	DATE CLAIM WAS INCURRED, NATURE OF LIEN , AND DESCRIPTION AND VALUE OF PROPERTY SUBJECT TO LIEN	CONTINGENT	UNLIQUIDATED	DISPUTED	AMOUNT OF CLAIM WITHOUT DEDUCTING VALUE OF COLLATERAL	UNSECURED PORTION, IF ANY
ACCOUNT NO.								
			VALUE $					
ACCOUNT NO.								
			VALUE $					
ACCOUNT NO.								
			VALUE $					
ACCOUNT NO.								
			VALUE $					
ACCOUNT NO.								
			VALUE $					

Sheet no._____of_ 0 _continuation sheets attached to Schedule of Creditors Holding Secured Claims

Subtotal (s)▶
(Total(s) of this page)

$

$

Total(s) ▶
(Use only on last page)

$

$

(Report also on Summary of Schedules.)

(If applicable, report also on Statistical Summary of Certain Liabilities and Related Data.)

B 6E (Official Form 6E) (12/07)

In re Sample, Joseph Allan Jr. and Sample ,   Case No._____
          ―――――――――――――――――――――
                    Debtor   **(if known)**

SCHEDULE E - CREDITORS HOLDING UNSECURED PRIORITY CLAIMS

A complete list of claims entitled to priority, listed separately by type of priority, is to be set forth on the sheets provided. Only holders of unsecured claims entitled to priority should be listed in this schedule. In the boxes provided on the attached sheets, state the name, mailing address, including zip code, and last four digits of the account number, if any, of all entities holding priority claims against the debtor or the property of the debtor, as of the date of the filing of the petition. Use a separate continuation sheet for each type of priority and label each with the type of priority.

The complete account number of any account the debtor has with the creditor is useful to the trustee and the creditor and may be provided if the debtor chooses to do so. If a minor child is a creditor, state the child's initials and the name and address of the child's parent or guardian, such as "A.B., a minor child, by John Doe, guardian." Do not disclose the child's name. See, 11 U.S.C. §112 and Fed. R. Bankr. P. 1007(m).

If any entity other than a spouse in a joint case may be jointly liable on a claim, place an "X" in the column labeled "Codebtor," include the entity on the appropriate schedule of creditors, and complete Schedule H-Codebtors. If a joint petition is filed, state whether the husband, wife, both of them, or the marital community may be liable on each claim by placing an "H," "W," "J." or "C" in the column labeled "Husband, Wife, Joint, or Community."   If the claim is contingent, place an "X" in the column labeled "Contingent." If the claim is unliquidated, place an "X" in the column labeled "Unliquidated." If the claim is disputed, place an "X" in the column labeled "Disputed." (You may need to place an "X" in more than one of these three columns.)

Report the total of claims listed on each sheet in the box labeled "Subtotals" on each sheet. Report the total of all claims listed on this Schedule E in the box labeled "Total" on the last sheet of the completed schedule. Report this total also on the Summary of Schedules.

Report the total of amounts entitled to priority listed on each sheet in the box labeled "Subtotals" on each sheet. Report the total of all amounts entitled to priority listed on this Schedule E in the box labeled "Totals" on the last sheet of the completed schedule. Individual debtors with primarily consumer debts report this total also on the Statistical Summary of Certain Liabilities and Related Data.

Report the total of amounts not entitled to priority listed on each sheet in the box labeled "Subtotals" on each sheet. Report the total of all amounts not entitled to priority listed on this Schedule E in the box labeled "Totals" on the last sheet of the completed schedule. Individual debtors with primarily consumer debts report this total also on the Statistical Summary of Certain Liabilities and Related Data.

☐ Check this box if debtor has no creditors holding unsecured priority claims to report on this Schedule E.

TYPES OF PRIORITY CLAIMS (Check the appropriate box(es) below if claims in that category are listed on the attached sheets.)

☑ **Domestic Support Obligations**

Claims for domestic support that are owed to or recoverable by a spouse, former spouse, or child of the debtor, or the parent, legal guardian, or responsible relative of such a child, or a governmental unit to whom such a domestic support claim has been assigned to the extent provided in 11 U.S.C. § 507(a)(1).

☐ **Extensions of credit in an involuntary case**

Claims arising in the ordinary course of the debtor's business or financial affairs after the commencement of the case but before the earlier of the appointment of a trustee or the order for relief. 11 U.S.C. § 507(a)(3).

☐ **Wages, salaries, and commissions**

Wages, salaries, and commissions, including vacation, severance, and sick leave pay owing to employees and commissions owing to qualifying independent sales representatives up to $10,950* per person earned within 180 days immediately preceding the filing of the original petition, or the cessation of business, whichever occurred first, to the extent provided in 11 U.S.C. § 507(a)(4).

☐ **Contributions to employee benefit plans**

Money owed to employee benefit plans for services rendered within 180 days immediately preceding the filing of the original petition, or the cessation of business, whichever occurred first, to the extent provided in 11 U.S.C. § 507(a)(5).

B 6E (Official Form 6E) (12/07) – Cont.

In re _Sample, Joseph Allan Jr. and Sample, Jane_ ,   Case No._____
                    Debtor   **(if known)**

☐ **Certain farmers and fishermen**

Claims of certain farmers and fishermen, up to $5,400* per farmer or fisherman, against the debtor, as provided in 11 U.S.C. § 507(a)(6).

☐ **Deposits by individuals**

Claims of individuals up to $2,425* for deposits for the purchase, lease, or rental of property or services for personal, family, or household use, that were not delivered or provided. 11 U.S.C. § 507(a)(7).

☑ **Taxes and Certain Other Debts Owed to Governmental Units**

Taxes, customs duties, and penalties owing to federal, state, and local governmental units as set forth in 11 U.S.C. § 507(a)(8).

☐ **Commitments to Maintain the Capital of an Insured Depository Institution**

Claims based on commitments to the FDIC, RTC, Director of the Office of Thrift Supervision, Comptroller of the Currency, or Board of Governors of the Federal Reserve System, or their predecessors or successors, to maintain the capital of an insured depository institution. 11 U.S.C. § 507 (a)(9).

☐ **Claims for Death or Personal Injury While Debtor Was Intoxicated**

Claims for death or personal injury resulting from the operation of a motor vehicle or vessel while the debtor was intoxicated from using alcohol, a drug, or another substance. 11 U.S.C. § 507(a)(10).

* Amounts are subject to adjustment on April 1, 2010, and every three years thereafter with respect to cases commenced on or after the date of adjustment.

_____2___ continuation sheets attached

B 6E (Official Form 6E) (12/07) -- Cont.

In re Sample, Joseph Allan Jr. and Sample, Jane A ,   Case No. _____
             Debtor   **(if known)**

SCHEDULE E - CREDITORS HOLDING UNSECURED PRIORITY CLAIMS
(Continuation Sheet)

Domestic Support Obligations   **Type of Priority for Claims Listed on This Sheet**

CREDITOR'S NAME, MAILING ADDRESS INCLUDING ZIP CODE, AND ACCOUNT NUMBER (*See instructions above.*)	CODEBTOR	HUSBAND, WIFE, JOINT, OR COMMUNITY	DATE CLAIM WAS INCURRED AND CONSIDERATION FOR CLAIM	CONTINGENT	UNLIQUIDATED	DISPUTED	AMOUNT OF CLAIM	AMOUNT ENTITLED TO PRIORITY	AMOUNT NOT ENTITLED TO PRIORITY, IF ANY
Account No. Mother of First Child 123 Road Beverly Hills, CA 90210		H	child support - payments current				0.00	0.00	0.00
Account No. 									
Account No. 									
Account No. 									

Sheet no __1__ of __2__ continuation sheets attached to Schedule of
Creditors Holding Priority Claims

	Subtotals► (Totals of this page)	$ 0.00	$ 0.00	0.00
	Total► (Use only on last page of the completed Schedule E. Report also on the Summary of Schedules.)	$		
	Totals► (Use only on last page of the completed Schedule E. If applicable, report also on the Statistical Summary of Certain Liabilities and Related Data.)		$	$

B 6E (Official Form 6E) (12/07) – Cont.

In re Sample, Joseph Allan Jr. and Sample, Jane A ,   Case No. _____
                    Debtor   **(if known)**

SCHEDULE E - CREDITORS HOLDING UNSECURED PRIORITY CLAIMS
(Continuation Sheet)

Taxes   **Type of Priority for Claims Listed on This Sheet**

CREDITOR'S NAME, MAILING ADDRESS INCLUDING ZIP CODE, AND ACCOUNT NUMBER (See instructions above.)	CODEBTOR	HUSBAND, WIFE, JOINT, OR COMMUNITY	DATE CLAIM WAS INCURRED AND CONSIDERATION FOR CLAIM	CONTINGENT	UNLIQUIDATED	DISPUTED	AMOUNT OF CLAIM	AMOUNT ENTITLED TO PRIORITY	AMOUNT NOT ENTITLED TO PRIORITY, IF ANY
Account No. Soc. Sec. # Internal Revenue Service Insolvency Operation PO Box 21126 Philadelphia, PA 19114-0326		J	2008 Income taxes				1,000.00	1,000.00	0.00
Account No.									
Account No.									
Account No.									

Sheet no. 2 of 2 continuation sheets attached to Schedule of Creditors Holding Priority Claims

Subtotals▶ (Totals of this page) $ 1,000.00 $ 1,000.00   0.00

Total▶ (Use only on last page of the completed Schedule E. Report also on the Summary of Schedules.) $ 1,000.00

Totals▶ (Use only on last page of the completed Schedule E. If applicable, report also on the Statistical Summary of Certain Liabilities and Related Data.) $ 1,000.00 $ 0.00

B 6F (Official Form 6F) (12/07)

In re Sample, Joseph Allan Jr. and Sample, Jane A.,   Case No. _____
              Debtor   **(if known)**

SCHEDULE F - CREDITORS HOLDING UNSECURED NONPRIORITY CLAIMS

State the name, mailing address, including zip code, and last four digits of any account number, of all entities holding unsecured claims without priority against the debtor or the property of the debtor, as of the date of filing of the petition. The complete account number of any account the debtor has with the creditor is useful to the trustee and the creditor and may be provided if the debtor chooses to do so. If a minor child is a creditor, state the child's initials and the name and address of the child's parent or guardian, such as "A.B., a minor child, by John Doe, guardian." Do not disclose the child's name. See, 11 U.S.C. §112 and Fed. R. Bankr. P. 1007(m). Do not include claims listed in Schedules D and E. If all creditors will not fit on this page, use the continuation sheet provided.

If any entity other than a spouse in a joint case may be jointly liable on a claim, place an "X" in the column labeled "Codebtor," include the entity on the appropriate schedule of creditors, and complete Schedule H - Codebtors. If a joint petition is filed, state whether the husband, wife, both of them, or the marital community may be liable on each claim by placing an "H," "W," "J," or "C" in the column labeled "Husband, Wife, Joint, or Community."

If the claim is contingent, place an "X" in the column labeled "Contingent." If the claim is unliquidated, place an "X" in the column labeled "Unliquidated." If the claim is disputed, place an "X" in the column labeled "Disputed." (You may need to place an "X" in more than one of these three columns.)

Report the total of all claims listed on this schedule in the box labeled "Total" on the last sheet of the completed schedule. Report this total also on the Summary of Schedules and, if the debtor is an individual with primarily consumer debts, report this total also on the Statistical Summary of Certain Liabilities and Related Data..

☐ Check this box if debtor has no creditors holding unsecured claims to report on this Schedule F.

CREDITOR'S NAME, MAILING ADDRESS INCLUDING ZIP CODE, AND ACCOUNT NUMBER *(See instructions above.)*	CODEBTOR	HUSBAND, WIFE, JOINT, OR COMMUNITY	DATE CLAIM WAS INCURRED AND CONSIDERATION FOR CLAIM. IF CLAIM IS SUBJECT TO SETOFF, SO STATE.	CONTINGENT	UNLIQUIDATED	DISPUTED	AMOUNT OF CLAIM
ACCOUNT NO. 1234 Bank of America PO Box 15184 Wilmington DE 19850-5184		J	2009 credit card				20,000.00
ACCOUNT NO. 1234 Chase PO Box 100018 Kennesaw, GA 30156		J	2009 credit card				10,000.00
ACCOUNT NO.							
ACCOUNT NO.							
				Subtotal▶		$	30,000.00

_0_ continuation sheets attached

                                                         Total▶ $ 30,000.00

(Use only on last page of the completed Schedule F.)
(Report also on Summary of Schedules and, if applicable, on the Statistical Summary of Certain Liabilities and Related Data.)

B 6F (Official Form 6F) (12/07) - Cont.

In re Sample, Joseph Allan Jr. and Sample, Jane A,   Case No. _____
              Debtor   **(if known)**

SCHEDULE F - CREDITORS HOLDING UNSECURED NONPRIORITY CLAIMS
(Continuation Sheet)

CREDITOR'S NAME, MAILING ADDRESS INCLUDING ZIP CODE, AND ACCOUNT NUMBER (See instructions above.)	CODEBTOR	HUSBAND, WIFE, JOINT, OR COMMUNITY	DATE CLAIM WAS INCURRED AND CONSIDERATION FOR CLAIM. IF CLAIM IS SUBJECT TO SETOFF, SO STATE.	CONTINGENT	UNLIQUIDATED	DISPUTED	AMOUNT OF CLAIM
ACCOUNT NO.							
ACCOUNT NO.							
ACCOUNT NO.							
ACCOUNT NO.							
ACCOUNT NO.							

Sheet no._____ of __0__ continuation sheets attached
to Schedule of Creditors Holding Unsecured
Nonpriority Claims

                                   Subtotal▶ $

                                       Total▶ $
(Use only on last page of the completed Schedule F.)
(Report also on Summary of Schedules and, if applicable on the Statistical
Summary of Certain Liabilities and Related Data.)

B 6G (Official Form 6G) (12/07)

In re Sample, Joseph Allan Jr. and Sample, Ja ,   Case No._____
                 Debtor   **(if known)**

SCHEDULE G - EXECUTORY CONTRACTS AND UNEXPIRED LEASES

Describe all executory contracts of any nature and all unexpired leases of real or personal property. Include any timeshare interests. State nature of debtor's interest in contract, i.e., "Purchaser," "Agent," etc. State whether debtor is the lessor or lessee of a lease. Provide the names and complete mailing addresses of all other parties to each lease or contract described. If a minor child is a party to one of the leases or contracts, state the child's initials and the name and address of the child's parent or guardian, such as "A.B., a minor child, by John Doe, guardian." Do not disclose the child's name. See, 11 U.S.C. §112 and Fed. R. Bankr. P. 1007(m).

☐ Check this box if debtor has no executory contracts or unexpired leases.

NAME AND MAILING ADDRESS, INCLUDING ZIP CODE, OF OTHER PARTIES TO LEASE OR CONTRACT.	DESCRIPTION OF CONTRACT OR LEASE AND NATURE OF DEBTOR'S INTEREST. STATE WHETHER LEASE IS FOR NONRESIDENTIAL REAL PROPERTY. STATE CONTRACT NUMBER OF ANY GOVERNMENT CONTRACT.
Ford Motor Credit Corporation PO Box 537901 Livonia, MI 48153	lease of 2009 Ford Fusion, $230 per month payments current, expires June 2011

B 6H (Official Form 6H) (12/07)

In re   Sample, Joseph Allan Jr. and Sample, ,   Case No. _____
         Debtor   **(if known)**

SCHEDULE H - CODEBTORS

Provide the information requested concerning any person or entity, other than a spouse in a joint case, that is also liable on any debts listed by the debtor in the schedules of creditors. Include all guarantors and co-signers. If the debtor resides or resided in a community property state, commonwealth, or territory (including Alaska, Arizona, California, Idaho, Louisiana, Nevada, New Mexico, Puerto Rico, Texas, Washington, or Wisconsin) within the eight-year period immediately preceding the commencement of the case, identify the name of the debtor's spouse and of any former spouse who resides or resided with the debtor in the community property state, commonwealth, or territory. Include all names used by the nondebtor spouse during the eight years immediately preceding the commencement of this case. If a minor child is a codebtor or a creditor, state the child's initials and the name and address of the child's parent or guardian, such as "A.B., a minor child, by John Doe, guardian." Do not disclose the child's name. See, 11 U.S.C. §112 and Fed. R. Bankr. P. 1007(m).

☐   Check this box if debtor has no codebtors.

NAME AND ADDRESS OF CODEBTOR	NAME AND ADDRESS OF CREDITOR
Joe Sample 123 Street Beverly Hills, CA 90210	Bank of America PO Box 15184 Wilmington, DE 19850-5184

B6I (Official Form 6I) (12/07)

In re <u>Sample, Joseph Allan Jr. and Sample, Ja</u> ,   Case No. _____
          Debtor   (if known)

SCHEDULE I - CURRENT INCOME OF INDIVIDUAL DEBTOR(S)

The column labeled "Spouse" must be completed in all cases filed by joint debtors and by every married debtor, whether or not a joint petition is filed, unless the spouses are separated and a joint petition is not filed. Do not state the name of any minor child. The average monthly income calculated on this form may differ from the current monthly income calculated on Form 22A, 22B, or 22C.

Debtor's Marital Status:	DEPENDENTS OF DEBTOR AND SPOUSE	
	RELATIONSHIP(S): Son, 2 daughters	AGE(S): 10, 5, 2

Employment:	DEBTOR	SPOUSE
Occupation	Carpenter	cashier
Name of Employer	Self-employed	Home Depot
How long employed	5 years	5 years
Address of Employer	123 Avenue Beverly Hills, CA 90210	PO Box 6029 The Lakes, NV 88901-6029

INCOME: (Estimate of average or projected monthly income at time case filed)

	DEBTOR	SPOUSE
1. Monthly gross wages, salary, and commissions (Prorate if not paid monthly)	$_____	$ 2,000.00
2. Estimate monthly overtime	$_____	$_____
3. SUBTOTAL	$_____	$ 2,000.00
4. LESS PAYROLL DEDUCTIONS		
a. Payroll taxes and social security	$_____	$ 500.00
b. Insurance	$_____	$ 200.00
c. Union dues	$_____	$_____
d. Other (Specify): _____	$_____	$_____
5. SUBTOTAL OF PAYROLL DEDUCTIONS	$_____	$ 700.00
6. TOTAL NET MONTHLY TAKE HOME PAY	$_____	$ 1,300.00
7. Regular income from operation of business or profession or farm (Attach detailed statement)	$ 2,000.00	$_____
8. Income from real property	$_____	$_____
9. Interest and dividends	$_____	$_____
10. Alimony, maintenance or support payments payable to the debtor for the debtor's use or that of dependents listed above	$_____	$_____
11. Social security or government assistance (Specify): _____	$_____	$_____
12. Pension or retirement income	$_____	$_____
13. Other monthly income (Specify): _____	$_____	$_____
14. SUBTOTAL OF LINES 7 THROUGH 13	$ 2,000.00	$ 0.00
15. AVERAGE MONTHLY INCOME (Add amounts on lines 6 and 14)	$ 2,000.00	$ 1,300.00
16. COMBINED AVERAGE MONTHLY INCOME: (Combine column totals from line 15)		$ 3,300.00

(Report also on Summary of Schedules and, if applicable, on Statistical Summary of Certain Liabilities and Related Data)

17. Describe any increase or decrease in income reasonably anticipated to occur within the year following the filing of this document:

B6J (Official Form 6J) (12/07)

In re Sample, Joseph Allan Jr. and Sample, , Case No. _____
      Debtor   **(if known)**

SCHEDULE J - CURRENT EXPENDITURES OF INDIVIDUAL DEBTOR(S)

Complete this schedule by estimating the average or projected monthly expenses of the debtor and the debtor's family at time case filed. Prorate any payments made bi-weekly, quarterly, semi-annually, or annually to show monthly rate. The average monthly expenses calculated on this form may differ from the deductions from income allowed on Form22A or 22C.

☐ Check this box if a joint petition is filed and debtor's spouse maintains a separate household. Complete a separate schedule of expenditures labeled "Spouse."

1. Rent or home mortgage payment (include lot rented for mobile home)		$ 1,000.00
a. Are real estate taxes included? Yes ✔ No _____		
b. Is property insurance included? Yes ✔ No _____		
2. Utilities: a. Electricity and heating fuel		$ 200.00
b. Water and sewer		$ 50.00
c. Telephone		$ 100.00
d. Other cell phones, cable and internet		$ 200.00
3. Home maintenance (repairs and upkeep)		$ 50.00
4. Food		$ 500.00
5. Clothing		$ 50.00
6. Laundry and dry cleaning		$ 30.00
7. Medical and dental expenses		$ 40.00
8. Transportation (not including car payments)		$ 200.00
9. Recreation, clubs and entertainment, newspapers, magazines, etc.		$ 0.00
10. Charitable contributions		$ 0.00
11. Insurance (not deducted from wages or included in home mortgage payments)		
a. Homeowner's or renter's		$ 0.00
b. Life		$ 0.00
c. Health		$ 0.00
d. Auto		$ 100.00
e. Other _____		$ 0.00
12. Taxes (not deducted from wages or included in home mortgage payments) (Specify) _____		$ 0.00
13. Installment payments: (In chapter 11, 12, and 13 cases, do not list payments to be included in the plan)		
a. Auto		$ 300.00
b. Other Auto 2		$ 230.00
c. Other 2nd mortgage		$ 150.00
14. Alimony, maintenance, and support paid to others		$ 0.00
15. Payments for support of additional dependents not living at your home		$ 100.00
16. Regular expenses from operation of business, profession, or farm (attach detailed statement)		$ 0.00
17. Other _____		$ 0.00
18. AVERAGE MONTHLY EXPENSES (Total lines 1-17. Report also on Summary of Schedules and, if applicable, on the Statistical Summary of Certain Liabilities and Related Data.)		$ 3,300.00

19. Describe any increase or decrease in expenditures reasonably anticipated to occur within the year following the filing of this document:

20. STATEMENT OF MONTHLY NET INCOME

a. Average monthly income from Line 15 of Schedule I	$ 3,300.00
b. Average monthly expenses from Line 18 above	$ 3,300.00
c. Monthly net income (a. minus b.)	$ 0.00

B6 Declaration (Official Form 6 - Declaration) (12/07)

In re **Sample, Joseph Allan Jr. and S** ,
　　　Debtor

Case No. _____
　　　　　　　(if known)

DECLARATION CONCERNING DEBTOR'S SCHEDULES

DECLARATION UNDER PENALTY OF PERJURY BY INDIVIDUAL DEBTOR

I declare under penalty of perjury that I have read the foregoing summary and schedules, consisting of __18__ sheets, and that they are true and correct to the best of my knowledge, information, and belief.

Date _____

Signature: _____
　　　　　　　　　　　Debtor

Date _____

Signature: _____
　　　　　　　　　(Joint Debtor, if any)

[If joint case, both spouses must sign.]

DECLARATION AND SIGNATURE OF NON-ATTORNEY BANKRUPTCY PETITION PREPARER (See 11 U.S.C. § 110)

I declare under penalty of perjury that: (1) I am a bankruptcy petition preparer as defined in 11 U.S.C. § 110; (2) I prepared this document for compensation and have provided the debtor with a copy of this document and the notices and information required under 11 U.S.C. §§ 110(b), 110(h) and 342(b); and, (3) if rules or guidelines have been promulgated pursuant to 11 U.S.C. § 110(h) setting a maximum fee for services chargeable by bankruptcy petition preparers, I have given the debtor notice of the maximum amount before preparing any document for filing for a debtor or accepting any fee from the debtor, as required by that section.

_____
Printed or Typed Name and Title, if any,
of Bankruptcy Petition Preparer

Social Security No. _____
(Required by 11 U.S.C. § 110.)

If the bankruptcy petition preparer is not an individual, state the name, title (if any), address, and social security number of the officer, principal, responsible person, or partner who signs this document.

_____
_____
_____
Address

X _____
Signature of Bankruptcy Petition Preparer

Date _____

Names and Social Security numbers of all other individuals who prepared or assisted in preparing this document, unless the bankruptcy petition preparer is not an individual:

If more than one person prepared this document, attach additional signed sheets conforming to the appropriate Official Form for each person.

A bankruptcy petition preparer's failure to comply with the provisions of title 11 and the Federal Rules of Bankruptcy Procedure may result in fines or imprisonment or both. 11 U.S.C. § 110; 18 U.S.C. § 156.

DECLARATION UNDER PENALTY OF PERJURY ON BEHALF OF A CORPORATION OR PARTNERSHIP

I, the _____ [the president or other officer or an authorized agent of the corporation or a member or an authorized agent of the partnership] of the _____ [corporation or partnership] named as debtor in this case, declare under penalty of perjury that I have read the foregoing summary and schedules, consisting of __18__ sheets (*Total shown on summary page plus 1*), and that they are true and correct to the best of my knowledge, information, and belief.

Date _____

Signature: _____

_____
[Print or type name of individual signing on behalf of debtor.]

[An individual signing on behalf of a partnership or corporation must indicate position or relationship to debtor.]

Penalty for making a false statement or concealing property: Fine of up to $500,000 or imprisonment for up to 5 years or both. 18 U.S.C. §§ 152 and 3571.

B 7 (Official Form 7) (12/07)

UNITED STATES BANKRUPTCY COURT

Southern District of California

In re: <u>Sample, Joseph Allan Jr. and Sample,</u>   Case No. _____
              Debtor   (if known)

STATEMENT OF FINANCIAL AFFAIRS

   This statement is to be completed by every debtor. Spouses filing a joint petition may file a single statement on which the information for both spouses is combined. If the case is filed under chapter 12 or chapter 13, a married debtor must furnish information for both spouses whether or not a joint petition is filed, unless the spouses are separated and a joint petition is not filed. An individual debtor engaged in business as a sole proprietor, partner, family farmer, or self-employed professional, should provide the information requested on this statement concerning all such activities as well as the individual's personal affairs. To indicate payments, transfers and the like to minor children, state the child's initials and the name and address of the child's parent or guardian, such as "A.B., a minor child, by John Doe, guardian." Do not disclose the child's name. See, 11 U.S.C. §112 and Fed. R. Bankr. P. 1007(m).

   Questions 1 - 18 are to be completed by all debtors. Debtors that are or have been in business, as defined below, also must complete Questions 19 - 25. **If the answer to an applicable question is "None," mark the box labeled "None."** If additional space is needed for the answer to any question, use and attach a separate sheet properly identified with the case name, case number (if known), and the number of the question.

DEFINITIONS

   "In business." A debtor is "in business" for the purpose of this form if the debtor is a corporation or partnership. An individual debtor is "in business" for the purpose of this form if the debtor is or has been, within six years immediately preceding the filing of this bankruptcy case, any of the following: an officer, director, managing executive, or owner of 5 percent or more of the voting or equity securities of a corporation; a partner, other than a limited partner, of a partnership; a sole proprietor or self-employed full-time or part-time. An individual debtor also may be "in business" for the purpose of this form if the debtor engages in a trade, business, or other activity, other than as an employee, to supplement income from the debtor's primary employment.

   "Insider." The term "insider" includes but is not limited to: relatives of the debtor; general partners of the debtor and their relatives; corporations of which the debtor is an officer, director, or person in control; officers, directors, and any owner of 5 percent or more of the voting or equity securities of a corporate debtor and their relatives; affiliates of the debtor and insiders of such affiliates; any managing agent of the debtor. 11 U.S.C. § 101.

---

  1. Income from employment or operation of business

None
☐
  State the gross amount of income the debtor has received from employment, trade, or profession, or from operation of the debtor's business, including part-time activities either as an employee or in independent trade or business, from the beginning of this calendar year to the date this case was commenced. State also the gross amounts received during the two years immediately preceding this calendar year. (A debtor that maintains, or has maintained, financial records on the basis of a fiscal rather than a calendar year may report fiscal year income. Identify the beginning and ending dates of the debtor's fiscal year.) If a joint petition is filed, state income for each spouse separately. (Married debtors filing under chapter 12 or chapter 13 must state income of both spouses whether or not a joint petition is filed, unless the spouses are separated and a joint petition is not filed.)

     AMOUNT   SOURCE

       $48000 - 2008 gross income $48000 - 2008 gross income
       $12000 - 2010 ytd gross wages to wife from Home Depot

2. Income other than from employment or operation of business

None ☑

State the amount of income received by the debtor other than from employment, trade, profession, operation of the debtor's business during the **two years** immediately preceding the commencement of this case. Give particulars. If a joint petition is filed, state income for each spouse separately. (Married debtors filing under chapter 12 or chapter 13 must state income for each spouse whether or not a joint petition is filed, unless the spouses are separated and a joint petition is not filed.)

AMOUNT	SOURCE

---

3. Payments to creditors

Complete a. or b., as appropriate, and c.

None ☐

a. *Individual or joint debtor(s) with primarily consumer debts:* List all payments on loans, installment purchases of goods or services, and other debts to any creditor made within **90 days** immediately preceding the commencement of this case unless the aggregate value of all property that constitutes or is affected by such transfer is less than $600. Indicate with an asterisk (*) any payments that were made to a creditor on account of a domestic support obligation or as part of an alternative repayment schedule under a plan by an approved nonprofit budgeting and credit counseling agency. (Married debtors filing under chapter 12 or chapter 13 must include payments by either or both spouses whether or not a joint petition is filed, unless the spouses are separated and a joint petition is not filed.)

NAME AND ADDRESS OF CREDITOR	DATES OF PAYMENTS	AMOUNT PAID	AMOUNT STILL OWING
Bank of America PO Box 15184, Wilmington, DE 19850	06/04/2010	1,000.00	20,000.00

None ☑

b. *Debtor whose debts are not primarily consumer debts: List each payment or other transfer to any creditor made* within **90 days** immediately preceding the commencement of the case unless the aggregate value of all property that constitutes or is affected by such transfer is less than $5,475. If the debtor is an individual, indicate with an asterisk (*) any payments that were made to a creditor on account of a domestic support obligation or as part of an alternative repayment schedule under a plan by an approved nonprofit budgeting and credit counseling agency. (Married debtors filing under chapter 12 or chapter 13 must include payments and other transfers by either or both spouses whether or not a joint petition is filed, unless the spouses are separated and a joint petition is not filed.)

NAME AND ADDRESS OF CREDITOR	DATES OF PAYMENTS/ TRANSFERS	AMOUNT PAID OR VALUE OF TRANSFERS	AMOUNT STILL OWING

None
☑   c. *All debtors:* List all payments made within **one year** immediately preceding the commencement of this case
     to or for the benefit of creditors who are or were insiders. (Married debtors filing under chapter 12 or chapter 13 must
     include payments by either or both spouses whether or not a joint petition is filed, unless the spouses are separated and
     a joint petition is not filed.)

NAME AND ADDRESS OF CREDITOR AND RELATIONSHIP TO DEBTOR	DATE OF PAYMENT	AMOUNT PAID	AMOUNT STILL OWING

---

4. Suits and administrative proceedings, executions, garnishments and attachments

None
☐   a. List all suits and administrative proceedings to which the debtor is or was a party within **one year** immediately
     preceding the filing of this bankruptcy case. (Married debtors filing under chapter 12 or chapter 13 must include
     information concerning either or both spouses whether or not a joint petition is filed, unless the spouses are separated
     and a joint petition is not filed.)

CAPTION OF SUIT AND CASE NUMBER	NATURE OF PROCEEDING	COURT OR AGENCY AND LOCATION	STATUS OR DISPOSITION
Chase v. Sample, Case no. 10-12345	collections action	Los Angeles District Court, Los Angeles,	pending

None
☑   b. Describe all property that has been attached, garnished or seized under any legal or equitable process within **one
     year** immediately preceding the commencement of this case. (Married debtors filing under chapter 12 or chapter 13
     must include information concerning property of either or both spouses whether or not a joint petition is filed, unless
     the spouses are separated and a joint petition is not filed.)

NAME AND ADDRESS OF PERSON FOR WHOSE BENEFIT PROPERTY WAS SEIZED	DATE OF SEIZURE	DESCRIPTION AND VALUE OF PROPERTY

---

5. Repossessions, foreclosures and returns

None
☑   List all property that has been repossessed by a creditor, sold at a foreclosure sale, transferred through a deed in lieu
     of foreclosure or returned to the seller, within **one year** immediately preceding the commencement of this case.
     (Married debtors filing under chapter 12 or chapter 13 must include information concerning property of either or both
     spouses whether or not a joint petition is filed, unless the spouses are separated and a joint petition is not filed.)

NAME AND ADDRESS OF CREDITOR OR SELLER	DATE OF REPOSSESSION, FORECLOSURE SALE, TRANSFER OR RETURN	DESCRIPTION AND VALUE OF PROPERTY

4

6. Assignments and receiverships

None ☑   a. Describe any assignment of property for the benefit of creditors made within **120 days** immediately preceding the commencement of this case. (Married debtors filing under chapter 12 or chapter 13 must include any assignment by either or both spouses whether or not a joint petition is filed, unless the spouses are separated and a joint petition is not filed.)

NAME AND ADDRESS OF ASSIGNEE	DATE OF ASSIGNMENT	TERMS OF ASSIGNMENT OR SETTLEMENT

None ☑   b. List all property which has been in the hands of a custodian, receiver, or court-appointed official within **one year** immediately preceding the commencement of this case. (Married debtors filing under chapter 12 or chapter 13 must include information concerning property of either or both spouses whether or not a joint petition is filed, unless the spouses are separated and a joint petition is not filed.)

NAME AND ADDRESS OF CUSTODIAN	NAME AND LOCATION OF COURT CASE TITLE & NUMBER	DATE OF ORDER	DESCRIPTION AND VALUE Of PROPERTY

7. Gifts

None ☐   List all gifts or charitable contributions made within **one year** immediately preceding the commencement of this case except ordinary and usual gifts to family members aggregating less than $200 in value per individual family member and charitable contributions aggregating less than $100 per recipient. (Married debtors filing under chapter 12 or chapter 13 must include gifts or contributions by either or both spouses whether or not a joint petition is filed, unless the spouses are separated and a joint petition is not filed.)

NAME AND ADDRESS OF PERSON OR ORGANIZATION	RELATIONSHIP TO DEBTOR, IF ANY	DATE OF GIFT	DESCRIPTION AND VALUE OF GIFT
Church 123 Boulevard, Beverly Hills, CA	none		$20 per week

8. Losses

None ☑   List all losses from fire, theft, other casualty or gambling within **one year** immediately preceding the commencement of this case **or since the commencement of this case**. (Married debtors filing under chapter 12 or chapter 13 must include losses by either or both spouses whether or not a joint petition is filed, unless the spouses are separated and a joint petition is not filed.)

DESCRIPTION AND VALUE OF PROPERTY	DESCRIPTION OF CIRCUMSTANCES AND, IF LOSS WAS COVERED IN WHOLE OR IN PART BY INSURANCE, GIVE PARTICULARS	DATE OF LOSS

5

9. Payments related to debt counseling or bankruptcy

None
☐

List all payments made or property transferred by or on behalf of the debtor to any persons, including attorneys, for consultation concerning debt consolidation, relief under the bankruptcy law or preparation of a petition in bankruptcy within **one year** immediately preceding the commencement of this case.

NAME AND ADDRESS OF PAYEE	DATE OF PAYMENT, NAME OF PAYER IF OTHER THAN DEBTOR	AMOUNT OF MONEY OR DESCRIPTION AND VALUE OF PROPERTY
CIN Legal Data Services 4540 Honeywell Court, Dayton, OH	6/12/2010	$30 for credit counseling

10. Other transfers

None
☐

a. List all other property, other than property transferred in the ordinary course of the business or financial affairs of the debtor, transferred either absolutely or as security within **two years** immediately preceding the commencement of this case. (Married debtors filing under chapter 12 or chapter 13 must include transfers by either or both spouses whether or not a joint petition is filed, unless the spouses are separated and a joint petition is not filed.)

NAME AND ADDRESS OF TRANSFEREE, RELATIONSHIP TO DEBTOR	DATE	DESCRIBE PROPERTY TRANSFERRED AND VALUE RECEIVED
Ford Dealership - none	06/01/2008	2002 Ford Escape, traded in

None
☑

b. List all property transferred by the debtor within **ten years** immediately preceding the commencement of this case to a self-settled trust or similar device of which the debtor is a beneficiary.

NAME OF TRUST OR OTHER DEVICE	DATE(S) OF TRANSFER(S)	AMOUNT OF MONEY OR DESCRIPTION AND VALUE OF PROPERTY OR DEBTOR'S INTEREST IN PROPERTY

11. Closed financial accounts

None
☑

List all financial accounts and instruments held in the name of the debtor or for the benefit of the debtor which were closed, sold, or otherwise transferred within **one year** immediately preceding the commencement of this case. Include checking, savings, or other financial accounts, certificates of deposit, or other instruments; shares and share accounts held in banks, credit unions, pension funds, cooperatives, associations, brokerage houses and other financial institutions. (Married debtors filing under chapter 12 or chapter 13 must include information concerning accounts or instruments held by or for either or both spouses whether or not a joint petition is filed, unless the spouses are separated and a joint petition is not filed.)

NAME AND ADDRESS OF INSTITUTION	TYPE OF ACCOUNT, LAST FOUR DIGITS OF ACCOUNT NUMBER, AND AMOUNT OF FINAL BALANCE	AMOUNT AND DATE OF SALE OR CLOSING

6

12. Safe deposit boxes

None
☑

List each safe deposit or other box or depository in which the debtor has or had securities, cash, or other valuables within **one year** immediately preceding the commencement of this case. (Married debtors filing under chapter 12 or chapter 13 must include boxes or depositories of either or both spouses whether or not a joint petition is filed, unless the spouses are separated and a joint petition is not filed.)

NAME AND ADDRESS OF BANK OR OTHER DEPOSITORY	NAMES AND ADDRESSES OF THOSE WITH ACCESS TO BOX OR DEPOSITORY	DESCRIPTION OF CONTENTS	DATE OF TRANSFER OR SURRENDER, IF ANY

13. Setoffs

None
☑

List all setoffs made by any creditor, including a bank, against a debt or deposit of the debtor within **90 days** preceding the commencement of this case. (Married debtors filing under chapter 12 or chapter 13 must include information concerning either or both spouses whether or not a joint petition is filed, unless the spouses are separated and a joint petition is not filed.)

NAME AND ADDRESS OF CREDITOR	DATE OF SETOFF	AMOUNT OF SETOFF

14. Property held for another person

None
☐

List all property owned by another person that the debtor holds or controls.

NAME AND ADDRESS OF OWNER	DESCRIPTION AND VALUE OF PROPERTY	LOCATION OF PROPERTY
Debtors' minor children 123 Avenue, Beverly Hills, CA	minor bank accounts, $500	Chase Bank

15. Prior address of debtor

None
☑

If debtor has moved within **three years** immediately preceding the commencement of this case, list all premises which the debtor occupied during that period and vacated prior to the commencement of this case. If a joint petition is filed, report also any separate address of either spouse.

ADDRESS	NAME USED	DATES OF OCCUPANCY

16. Spouses and Former Spouses

None ☐ If the debtor resides or resided in a community property state, commonwealth, or territory (including Alaska, Arizona, California, Idaho, Louisiana, Nevada, New Mexico, Puerto Rico, Texas, Washington, or Wisconsin) within **eight years** immediately preceding the commencement of the case, identify the name of the debtor's spouse and of any former spouse who resides or resided with the debtor in the community property state.

NAME
Mother of First Child

17. Environmental Information.

For the purpose of this question, the following definitions apply:

"Environmental Law" means any federal, state, or local statute or regulation regulating pollution, contamination, releases of hazardous or toxic substances, wastes or material into the air, land, soil, surface water, groundwater, or other medium, including, but not limited to, statutes or regulations regulating the cleanup of these substances, wastes, or material.

"Site" means any location, facility, or property as defined under any Environmental Law, whether or not presently or formerly owned or operated by the debtor, including, but not limited to, disposal sites.

"Hazardous Material" means anything defined as a hazardous waste, hazardous substance, toxic substance, hazardous material, pollutant, or contaminant or similar term under an Environmental Law.

None ☑ a. List the name and address of every site for which the debtor has received notice in writing by a governmental unit that it may be liable or potentially liable under or in violation of an Environmental Law. Indicate the governmental unit, the date of the notice, and, if known, the Environmental Law:

SITE NAME AND ADDRESS	NAME AND ADDRESS OF GOVERNMENTAL UNIT	DATE OF NOTICE	ENVIRONMENTAL LAW

None ☑ b. List the name and address of every site for which the debtor provided notice to a governmental unit of a release of Hazardous Material. Indicate the governmental unit to which the notice was sent and the date of the notice.

SITE NAME AND ADDRESS	NAME AND ADDRESS OF GOVERNMENTAL UNIT	DATE OF NOTICE	ENVIRONMENTAL LAW

None ☑ c. List all judicial or administrative proceedings, including settlements or orders, under any Environmental Law with respect to which the debtor is or was a party. Indicate the name and address of the governmental unit that is or was a party to the proceeding, and the docket number.

NAME AND ADDRESS OF GOVERNMENTAL UNIT	DOCKET NUMBER	STATUS OR DISPOSITION

18 . Nature, location and name of business

None ☐ a. *If the debtor is an individual*, list the names, addresses, taxpayer-identification numbers, nature of the businesses, and beginning and ending dates of all businesses in which the debtor was an officer, director, partner, or managing

8

executive of a corporation, partner in a partnership, sole proprietor, or was self-employed in a trade, profession, or other activity either full- or part-time within **six years** immediately preceding the commencement of this case, or in which the debtor owned 5 percent or more of the voting or equity securities within **six years** immediately preceding the commencement of this case.

If the debtor is a partnership, list the names, addresses, taxpayer-identification numbers, nature of the businesses, and beginning and ending dates of all businesses in which the debtor was a partner or owned 5 percent or more of the voting or equity securities, within **six years** immediately preceding the commencement of this case.

If the debtor is a corporation, list the names, addresses, taxpayer-identification numbers, nature of the businesses, and beginning and ending dates of all businesses in which the debtor was a partner or owned 5 percent or more of the voting or equity securities within **six years** immediately preceding the commencement of this case.

NAME	LAST FOUR DIGITS OF SOCIAL-SECURITY OR OTHER INDIVIDUAL TAXPAYER-I.D. NO. (ITIN)/ COMPLETE EIN	ADDRESS	NATURE OF BUSINESS	BEGINNING AND ENDING DATES
Sample Business Inc.	6789	123 Avenue Beverly Hills	carpentry business	2008 to present

None ☑ b. Identify any business listed in response to subdivision a., above, that is "single asset real estate" as defined in 11 U.S.C. § 101.

NAME   ADDRESS

The following questions are to be completed by every debtor that is a corporation or partnership and by any individual debtor who is or has been, within **six years** immediately preceding the commencement of this case, any of the following: an officer, director, managing executive, or owner of more than 5 percent of the voting or equity securities of a corporation; a partner, other than a limited partner, of a partnership, a sole proprietor, or self-employed in a trade, profession, or other activity, either full- or part-time.

(An individual or joint debtor should complete this portion of the statement only if the debtor is or has been in business, as defined above, within six years immediately preceding the commencement of this case. A debtor who has not been in business within those six years should go directly to the signature page.)

---

19. Books, records and financial statements

None ☑ a. List all bookkeepers and accountants who within **two years** immediately preceding the filing of this bankruptcy case kept or supervised the keeping of books of account and records of the debtor.

NAME AND ADDRESS   DATES SERVICES RENDERED

None ☑ b. List all firms or individuals who within **two years** immediately preceding the filing of this bankruptcy case have audited the books of account and records, or prepared a financial statement of the debtor.

NAME   ADDRESS   DATES SERVICES RENDERED

None ☑ c. List all firms or individuals who at the time of the commencement of this case were in possession of the books of account and records of the debtor. If any of the books of account and records are not available, explain.

NAME   ADDRESS

None ☑ d. List all financial institutions, creditors and other parties, including mercantile and trade agencies, to whom a financial statement was issued by the debtor within **two years** immediately preceding the commencement of this case.

NAME AND ADDRESS   DATE ISSUED

---

20. Inventories

None ☑ a. List the dates of the last two inventories taken of your property, the name of the person who supervised the taking of each inventory, and the dollar amount and basis of each inventory.

		DOLLAR AMOUNT OF INVENTORY
DATE OF INVENTORY	INVENTORY SUPERVISOR	(Specify cost, market or other basis)

None ☑ b. List the name and address of the person having possession of the records of each of the inventories reported in a., above.

	NAME AND ADDRESSES OF CUSTODIAN
DATE OF INVENTORY	OF INVENTORY RECORDS

---

21 . Current Partners, Officers, Directors and Shareholders

None ☑ a. If the debtor is a partnership, list the nature and percentage of partnership interest of each member of the partnership.

NAME AND ADDRESS   NATURE OF INTEREST   PERCENTAGE OF INTEREST

None ☑ b.   If the debtor is a corporation, list all officers and directors of the corporation, and each stockholder who directly or indirectly owns, controls, or holds 5 percent or more of the voting or equity securities of the corporation.

		NATURE AND PERCENTAGE OF STOCK OWNERSHIP
NAME AND ADDRESS	TITLE	

10

22 . Former partners, officers, directors and shareholders

None
☑
a. If the debtor is a partnership, list each member who withdrew from the partnership within **one year** immediately preceding the commencement of this case.

NAME   ADDRESS   DATE OF WITHDRAWAL

None
☑
b. If the debtor is a corporation, list all officers or directors whose relationship with the corporation terminated within **one year** immediately preceding the commencement of this case.

NAME AND ADDRESS   TITLE   DATE OF TERMINATION

---

23 . Withdrawals from a partnership or distributions by a corporation

None
☑
If the debtor is a partnership or corporation, list all withdrawals or distributions credited or given to an insider, including compensation in any form, bonuses, loans, stock redemptions, options exercised and any other perquisite during **one year** immediately preceding the commencement of this case.

NAME & ADDRESS   AMOUNT OF MONEY
OF RECIPIENT,   DATE AND PURPOSE   OR DESCRIPTION
RELATIONSHIP TO DEBTOR   OF WITHDRAWAL   AND VALUE OF PROPERTY

---

24. Tax Consolidation Group.

None
☑
If the debtor is a corporation, list the name and federal taxpayer-identification number of the parent corporation of any consolidated group for tax purposes of which the debtor has been a member at any time within **six years** immediately preceding the commencement of the case.

NAME OF PARENT CORPORATION   TAXPAYER-IDENTIFICATION NUMBER (EIN)

---

25. Pension Funds.

None
☑
If the debtor is not an individual, list the name and federal taxpayer-identification number of any pension fund to which the debtor, as an employer, has been responsible for contributing at any time within **six years** immediately preceding the commencement of the case.

NAME OF PENSION FUND   TAXPAYER-IDENTIFICATION NUMBER (EIN)

* * * * * *

[If completed by an individual or individual and spouse]

I declare under penalty of perjury that I have read the answers contained in the foregoing statement of financial affairs and any attachments thereto and that they are true and correct.

Date _____

Signature
of Debtor _____

Date _____

Signature of
Joint Debtor
(if any) _____

[If completed on behalf of a partnership or corporation]

I declare under penalty of perjury that I have read the answers contained in the foregoing statement of financial affairs and any attachments thereto and that they are true and correct to the best of my knowledge, information and belief.

Date _____

Signature _____

Print Name and
Title _____

[An individual signing on behalf of a partnership or corporation must indicate position or relationship to debtor.]

_____continuation sheets attached

Penalty for making a false statement: Fine of up to $500,000 or imprisonment for up to 5 years, or both. 18 U.S.C. §§ 152 and 3571

DECLARATION AND SIGNATURE OF NON-ATTORNEY BANKRUPTCY PETITION PREPARER (See 11 U.S.C. § 110)

I declare under penalty of perjury that: (1) I am a bankruptcy petition preparer as defined in 11 U.S.C. § 110; (2) I prepared this document for compensation and have provided the debtor with a copy of this document and the notices and information required under 11 U.S.C. §§ 110(b), 110(h), and 342(b); and, (3) if rules or guidelines have been promulgated pursuant to 11 U.S.C. § 110(h) setting a maximum fee for services chargeable by bankruptcy petition preparers, I have given the debtor notice of the maximum amount before preparing any document for filing for a debtor or accepting any fee from the debtor, as required by that section.

Printed or Typed Name and Title, if any, of Bankruptcy Petition Preparer   Social-Security No. (Required by 11 U.S.C. § 110.)

If the bankruptcy petition preparer is not an individual, state the name, title (if any), address, and social-security number of the officer, principal, responsible person, or partner who signs this document.

Address _____

Signature of Bankruptcy Petition Preparer   Date

Names and Social-Security numbers of all other individuals who prepared or assisted in preparing this document unless the bankruptcy petition preparer is not an individual:

If more than one person prepared this document, attach additional signed sheets conforming to the appropriate Official Form for each person

A bankruptcy petition preparer's failure to comply with the provisions of title 11 and the Federal Rules of Bankruptcy Procedure may result in fines or imprisonment or both. 18 U.S.C. § 156.

Bank of America
PO Box 15184
Wilmington, DE 19850-5184

Chase
Attn: Bankruptcy Dept
Po Box 100018
Kennesaw, GA 30156

CitiMortgage
1000 Technology Drive
O Fallon, MO 63368

Ford Motor Credit Corporation
Ford Credit National Bankruptcy Center
Po Box 537901
Livonia, MI 48153

Internal Revenue Service
Insolvency Operation
PO Box 21126
Philadelphia, PA 19114-0326

Joe Sample
123 Street
Beverly Hills, CA 90210

Mother of First Child
123 Road
Beverly Hills, CA 90210

Toyota Motor Credit Co
5005 North River Blvd., NE
Cedar Rapids, IA 52411-6634

B 8 (Official Form 8) (12/08)

UNITED STATES BANKRUPTCY COURT

Southern District of California

In re Sample, Joseph Allan Jr. and S,   Case No. _____
_____
Debtor   Chapter 7

CHAPTER 7 INDIVIDUAL DEBTOR'S STATEMENT OF INTENTION

PART A – Debts secured by property of the estate. *(Part A must be fully completed for **EACH** debt which is secured by property of the estate. Attach additional pages if necessary.)*

Property No. 1	
Creditor's Name: Bank of America	**Describe Property Securing Debt:** Debtors' Homestead

Property will be *(check one)*:
    ☐ Surrendered   ☑ Retained

If retaining the property, I intend to *(check at least one)*:
    ☐ Redeem the property
    ☑ Reaffirm the debt
    ☐ Other. Explain _____ (for example, avoid lien using 11 U.S.C. § 522(f)).

Property is *(check one)*:
    ☑ Claimed as exempt   ☐ Not claimed as exempt

Property No. 2 *(if necessary)*	
Creditor's Name: CitiMortgage	**Describe Property Securing Debt:** Debtors' Homestead

Property will be *(check one)*:
    ☐ Surrendered   ☑ Retained

If retaining the property, I intend to *(check at least one)*:
    ☐ Redeem the property
    ☑ Reaffirm the debt
    ☐ Other. Explain _____ (for example, avoid lien using 11 U.S.C. § 522(f)).

Property is *(check one)*:
    ☑ Claimed as exempt   ☐ Not claimed as exempt

B 8 (Official Form 8) (12/08)   Page 2

PART B – Personal property subject to unexpired leases. *(All three columns of Part B must be completed for each unexpired lease. Attach additional pages if necessary.)*

Property No. 1		
Lessor's Name: Ford Motor Credit Co.	**Describe Leased Property:** 2009 Ford Fusion	Lease will be Assumed pursuant to 11 U.S.C. § 365(p)(2): ☑ YES ☐ NO

Property No. 2 *(if necessary)*		
Lessor's Name:	**Describe Leased Property:**	Lease will be Assumed pursuant to 11 U.S.C. § 365(p)(2): ☐ YES ☐ NO

Property No. 3 *(if necessary)*		
Lessor's Name:	**Describe Leased Property:**	Lease will be Assumed pursuant to 11 U.S.C. § 365(p)(2): ☐ YES ☐ NO

__1__ continuation sheets attached *(if any)*

I declare under penalty of perjury that the above indicates my intention as to any property of my estate securing a debt and/or personal property subject to an unexpired lease.

Date: _____   _____
                                 Signature of Debtor

                                 _____
                                 Signature of Joint Debtor

B 8 (Official Form 8) (12/08)   Page 3

CHAPTER 7 INDIVIDUAL DEBTOR'S STATEMENT OF INTENTION
(Continuation Sheet)

PART A - Continuation

Property No.	
Creditor's Name: Toyota Motor Credit Co.	**Describe Property Securing Debt:** 2006 Toyota Rav 4

Property will be *(check one)*:
    ☐ Surrendered   ☑ Retained

If retaining the property, I intend to *(check at least one)*:
    ☐ Redeem the property
    ☑ Reaffirm the debt
    ☐ Other. Explain _____ (for example, avoid lien
using 11 U.S.C. § 522(f)).

Property is *(check one)*:
    ☑ Claimed as exempt   ☐ Not claimed as exempt

PART B - Continuation

Property No.		
Lessor's Name:	**Describe Leased Property:**	Lease will be Assumed pursuant to 11 U.S.C. § 365(p)(2): ☐ YES ☐ NO

Property No.		
Lessor's Name:	**Describe Leased Property:**	Lease will be Assumed pursuant to 11 U.S.C. § 365(p)(2): ☐ YES ☐ NO

B 21 (Official Form 21) (12/07)

UNITED STATES BANKRUPTCY COURT
Southern District of California

In re Joseph Allan Sample, Jr; Jane Ann Sample   ,   )
    [Set forth here all names including married, maiden,   )
    and trade names used by debtor within last 8 years]   )
)
                  Debtor   ) Case No. _____
Address 123 Avenue   )
    Beverly Hills, CA 90210   ) Chapter 7 _____
)
Last four digits of Social-Security or Individual Taxpayer-)
Identification (ITIN) No(s)..(if any):   )
6789 & 5678   )
Employer Tax-Identification (EIN) No(s).(if any):)
)

STATEMENT OF SOCIAL-SECURITY NUMBER(S)
(or other Individual Taxpayer-Identification Number(s) (ITIN(s)))

1.Name of Debtor (Last, First, Middle): Sample, Joseph Allan Jr.
(Check the appropriate box and, if applicable, provide the required information.)

    ☑Debtor has a Social-Security Number and it is: 123-45-6789
        (If more than one, state all.)
    ☐ Debtor does not have a Social-Security Number but has an Individual Taxpayer-Identification
        Number (ITIN), and it is: _____
        (If more than one, state all.)
    ☐ Debtor does not have either a Social-Security Number or an Individual Taxpayer-Identification
        Number (ITIN).

2.Name of Joint Debtor (Last, First, Middle): Sample, Jane Ann
(Check the appropriate box and, if applicable, provide the required information.)

    ☑Joint Debtor has a Social-Security Number and it is: 012-34-5678
        (If more than one, state all.)
    ☐ Joint Debtor does not have a Social-Security Number but has an Individual Taxpayer-Identification
        Number (ITIN) and it is: _____
        (If more than one, state all.)
    ☐ Joint Debtor does not have either a Social-Security Number or an Individual Taxpayer-Identification
        Number (ITIN).

I declare under penalty of perjury that the foregoing is true and correct.

     X _____
       Signature of Debtor   Date
     X _____
       Signature of Joint Debtor   Date

---

* *Joint debtors must provide information for both spouses.*

Penalty for making a false statement: Fine of up to $250,000 or up to 5 years imprisonment or both. 18 U.S.C. §§ 152 and 3571.

B22A (Official Form 22A) (Chapter 7) (12/08)

In re **Sample, Joseph Allan Jr. and S**
                        Debtor(s)

Case Number: _____
                        (If known)

According to the information required to be entered on this statement (check one box as directed in Part I, III, or VI of this statement):

☐ **The presumption arises.**
☑ **The presumption does not arise.**
☐ **The presumption is temporarily inapplicable.**

CHAPTER 7 STATEMENT OF CURRENT MONTHLY INCOME AND MEANS-TEST CALCULATION

In addition to Schedules I and J, this statement must be completed by every individual chapter 7 debtor, whether or not filing jointly. Unless the exclusion in Line 1C applies, joint debtors may complete a single statement. If the exclusion in Line 1C applies, each joint filer must complete a separate statement.

Part I. MILITARY AND NON-CONSUMER DEBTORS	
1A	**Disabled Veterans.** If you are a disabled veteran described in the Declaration in this Part IA, (1) check the box at the beginning of the Declaration, (2) check the box for "The presumption does not arise" at the top of this statement, and (3) complete the verification in Part VIII. Do not complete any of the remaining parts of this statement. ☐ **Declaration of Disabled Veteran.** By checking this box, I declare under penalty of perjury that I am a disabled veteran (as defined in 38 U.S.C. § 3741(1)) whose indebtedness occurred primarily during a period in which I was on active duty (as defined in 10 U.S.C. § 101(d)(1)) or while I was performing a homeland defense activity (as defined in 32 U.S.C. §901(1)).
1B	**Non-consumer Debtors.** If your debts are not primarily consumer debts, check the box below and complete the verification in Part VIII. Do not complete any of the remaining parts of this statement. ☐ **Declaration of non-consumer debts.** By checking this box, I declare that my debts are not primarily consumer debts.

1C	**Reservists and National Guard Members; active duty or homeland defense activity.** Members of a reserve component of the Armed Forces and members of the National Guard who were called to active duty (as defined in 10 U.S.C. § 101(d)(1)) after September 11, 2001, for a period of at least 90 days, or who have performed homeland defense activity (as defined in 32 U.S.C. § 901(1)) for a period of at least 90 days, are excluded from all forms of means testing during the time of active duty or homeland defense activity and for 540 days thereafter (the "exclusion period"). If you qualify for this temporary exclusion, (1) check the appropriate boxes and complete any required information in the Declaration of Reservists and National Guard Members below, (2) check the box for "The presumption is temporarily inapplicable" at the top of this statement, and (3) complete the verification in Part VIII. **During your exclusion period you are not required to complete the balance of this form, but you must complete the form no later than 14 days after the date on which your exclusion period ends, unless the time for filing a motion raising the means test presumption expires in your case before your exclusion period ends.**
	
	☐ **Declaration of Reservists and National Guard Members.** By checking this box and making the appropriate entries below, I declare that I am eligible for a temporary exclusion from means testing because, as a member of a reserve component of the Armed Forces or the National Guard
	
	    a. ☐ I was called to active duty after September 11, 2001, for a period of at least 90 days and
	        ☐ I remain on active duty /or/
	        ☐ I was released from active duty on _____, which is less than 540 days before this bankruptcy case was filed;
	
	        OR
	
	    b. ☐ I am performing homeland defense activity for a period of at least 90 days /or/
	        ☐ I performed homeland defense activity for a period of at least 90 days, terminating on _____, which is less than 540 days before this bankruptcy case was filed.

B22A (Official Form 22A) (Chapter 7) (12/08)   2

	Part II. CALCULATION OF MONTHLY INCOME FOR § 707(b)(7) EXCLUSION		
2	**Marital/filing status.** Check the box that applies and complete the balance of this part of this statement as directed. a. ☐ Unmarried. **Complete only Column A ("Debtor's Income") for Lines 3-11.** b. ☐ Married, not filing jointly, with declaration of separate households. By checking this box, debtor declares under penalty of perjury: "My spouse and I are legally separated under applicable non-bankruptcy law or my spouse and I are living apart other than for the purpose of evading the requirements of § 707(b)(2)(A) of the Bankruptcy Code." **Complete only Column A ("Debtor's Income") for Lines 3-11.** c. ☐ Married, not filing jointly, without the declaration of separate households set out in Line 2.b above. **Complete both Column A ("Debtor's Income") and Column B ("Spouse's Income") for Lines 3-11.** d. ☑ Married, filing jointly. **Complete both Column A ("Debtor's Income") and Column B ("Spouse's Income") for Lines 3-11.**		
	All figures must reflect average monthly income received from all sources, derived during the six calendar months prior to filing the bankruptcy case, ending on the last day of the month before the filing. If the amount of monthly income varied during the six months, you must divide the six-month total by six, and enter the result on the appropriate line.	**Column A** Debtor's Income	**Column B** Spouse's Income
3	**Gross wages, salary, tips, bonuses, overtime, commissions.**	$ 0.00	$ 2,000.00
4	**Income from the operation of a business, profession or farm.** Subtract Line b from Line a and enter the difference in the appropriate column(s) of Line 4. If you operate more than one business, profession or farm, enter aggregate numbers and provide details on an attachment. Do not enter a number less than zero. **Do not include any part of the business expenses entered on Line b as a deduction in Part V.** a. Gross receipts $ 2,000.00 b. Ordinary and necessary business expenses $ 0.00 c. Business income Subtract Line b from Line a	$ 2,000.00	$ 0.00
5	**Rent and other real property income.** Subtract Line b from Line a and enter the difference in the appropriate column(s) of Line 5. Do not enter a number less than zero. **Do not include any part of the operating expenses entered on Line b as a deduction in Part V.** a. Gross receipts $ 0.00 b. Ordinary and necessary operating expenses $ 0.00 c. Rent and other real property income Subtract Line b from Line a	$ 0.00	$ 0.00
6	**Interest, dividends and royalties.**	$ 0.00	$ 0.00
7	**Pension and retirement income.**	$ 0.00	$ 0.00
8	**Any amounts paid by another person or entity, on a regular basis, for the household expenses of the debtor or the debtor's dependents, including child support paid for that purpose.** Do not include alimony or separate maintenance payments or amounts paid by your spouse if Column B is completed.	$ 0.00	$ 0.00
9	**Unemployment compensation.** Enter the amount in the appropriate column(s) of Line 9. However, if you contend that unemployment compensation received by you or your spouse was a benefit under the Social Security Act, do not list the amount of such compensation in Column A or B, but instead state the amount in the space below: Unemployment compensation claimed to be a benefit under the Social Security Act Debtor $ 0.00 Spouse $ 0.00	$ 0.00	$ 0.00

B22A (Official Form 22A) (Chapter 7) (12/08)   3

10	**Income from all other sources.** Specify source and amount. If necessary, list additional sources on a separate page. **Do not include alimony or separate maintenance payments paid by your spouse if Column B is completed, but include all other payments of alimony or separate maintenance.** Do not include any benefits received under the Social Security Act or payments received as a victim of a war crime, crime against humanity, or as a victim of international or domestic terrorism.		
	a. $ 0.00		
	b. 0 $ 0.00		
	Total and enter on Line 10	$ 0.00	$ 0.00
11	**Subtotal of Current Monthly Income for § 707(b)(7).** Add Lines 3 thru 10 in Column A, and, if Column B is completed, add Lines 3 through 10 in Column B. Enter the total(s).	$ 2,000.00	$ 2,000.00
12	**Total Current Monthly Income for § 707(b)(7).** If Column B has been completed, add Line 11, Column A to Line 11, Column B, and enter the total. If Column B has not been completed, enter the amount from Line 11, Column A.		$ 4,000.00

Part III. APPLICATION OF § 707(b)(7) EXCLUSION

13	**Annualized Current Monthly Income for § 707(b)(7).** Multiply the amount from Line 12 by the number 12 and enter the result.	$ 48,000.00
14	**Applicable median family income.** Enter the median family income for the applicable state and household size. (This information is available by family size at www.usdoj.gov/ust/ or from the clerk of the bankruptcy court.)	
	a. Enter debtor's state of residence: __CA__ b. Enter debtor's household size: ___4___	$ 79,477.00
15	**Application of Section 707(b)(7).** Check the applicable box and proceed as directed.	
	☑ **The amount on Line 13 is less than or equal to the amount on Line 14.** Check the box for "The presumption does not arise" at the top of page 1 of this statement, and complete Part VIII; do not complete Parts IV, V, VI or VII.	
	☐ **The amount on Line 13 is more than the amount on Line 14.** Complete the remaining parts of this statement.	

Complete Parts IV, V, VI, and VII of this statement only if required. (See Line 15.)

Part IV. CALCULATION OF CURRENT MONTHLY INCOME FOR § 707(b)(2)

16	**Enter the amount from Line 12.**	$ 4,000.00
17	**Marital adjustment.** If you checked the box at Line 2.c, enter on Line 17 the total of any income listed in Line 11, Column B that was NOT paid on a regular basis for the household expenses of the debtor or the debtor's dependents. Specify in the lines below the basis for excluding the Column B income (such as payment of the spouse's tax liability or the spouse's support of persons other than the debtor or the debtor's dependents) and the amount of income devoted to each purpose. If necessary, list additional adjustments on a separate page. If you did not check box at Line 2.c, enter zero.	
	a. $	
	b. $	
	c. $	
	Total and enter on Line 17.	$
18	**Current monthly income for § 707(b)(2).** Subtract Line 17 from Line 16 and enter the result.	$

Part V. CALCULATION OF DEDUCTIONS FROM INCOME

Subpart A: Deductions under Standards of the Internal Revenue Service (IRS)

19A	**National Standards: food, clothing and other items.** Enter in Line 19A the "Total" amount from IRS National Standards for Food, Clothing and Other Items for the applicable household size. (This information is available at www.usdoj.gov/ust/ or from the clerk of the bankruptcy court.)	$

B22A (Official Form 22A) (Chapter 7) (12/08)   4

19B	**National Standards: health care.** Enter in Line a1 below the amount from IRS National Standards for Out-of-Pocket Health Care for persons under 65 years of age, and in Line a2 the IRS National Standards for Out-of-Pocket Health Care for persons 65 years of age or older. (This information is available at www.usdoj.gov/ust/ or from the clerk of the bankruptcy court.) Enter in Line b1 the number of members of your household who are under 65 years of age, and enter in Line b2 the number of members of your household who are 65 years of age or older. (The total number of household members must be the same as the number stated in Line 14b.) Multiply Line a1 by Line b1 to obtain a total amount for household members under 65, and enter the result in Line c1. Multiply Line a2 by Line b2 to obtain a total amount for household members 65 and older, and enter the result in Line c2. Add Lines c1 and c2 to obtain a total health care amount, and enter the result in Line 19B.	

Household members under 65 years of age		Household members 65 years of age or older			
a1.	Allowance per member		a2.	Allowance per member	
b1.	Number of members		b2.	Number of members	
c1.	Subtotal		c2.	Subtotal		$

20A	**Local Standards: housing and utilities; non-mortgage expenses.** Enter the amount of the IRS Housing and Utilities Standards; non-mortgage expenses for the applicable county and household size. (This information is available at www.usdoj.gov/ust/ or from the clerk of the bankruptcy court).	$

20B	**Local Standards: housing and utilities; mortgage/rent expense.** Enter, in Line a below, the amount of the IRS Housing and Utilities Standards; mortgage/rent expense for your county and household size (this information is available at www.usdoj.gov/ust/ or from the clerk of the bankruptcy court); enter on Line b the total of the Average Monthly Payments for any debts secured by your home, as stated in Line 42; subtract Line b from Line a and enter the result in Line 20B. **Do not enter an amount less than zero.**	

a.	IRS Housing and Utilities Standards; mortgage/rental expense	$	
b.	Average Monthly Payment for any debts secured by your home, if any, as stated in Line 42	$	
c.	Net mortgage/rental expense	Subtract Line b from Line a.	$

21	**Local Standards: housing and utilities; adjustment.** If you contend that the process set out in Lines 20A and 20B does not accurately compute the allowance to which you are entitled under the IRS Housing and Utilities Standards, enter any additional amount to which you contend you are entitled, and state the basis for your contention in the space below:	
		$

22A	**Local Standards: transportation; vehicle operation/public transportation expense.** You are entitled to an expense allowance in this category regardless of whether you pay the expenses of operating a vehicle and regardless of whether you use public transportation. Check the number of vehicles for which you pay the operating expenses or for which the operating expenses are included as a contribution to your household expenses in Line 8. ☐ 0 ☐ 1 ☐ 2 or more. If you checked 0, enter on Line 22A the "Public Transportation" amount from IRS Local Standards: Transportation. If you checked 1 or 2 or more, enter on Line 22A the "Operating Costs" amount from IRS Local Standards: Transportation for the applicable number of vehicles in the applicable Metropolitan Statistical Area or Census Region. (These amounts are available at www.usdoj.gov/ust/ or from the clerk of the bankruptcy court.)	$

22B	**Local Standards: transportation; additional public transportation expense.** If you pay the operating expenses for a vehicle and also use public transportation, and you contend that you are entitled to an additional deduction for your public transportation expenses, enter on Line 22B the "Public Transportation" amount from IRS Local Standards: Transportation. (This amount is available at www.usdoj.gov/ust/ or from the clerk of the bankruptcy court.)	$

B22A (Official Form 22A) (Chapter 7) (12/08)   5

23	**Local Standards: transportation ownership/lease expense; Vehicle 1.** Check the number of vehicles for which you claim an ownership/lease expense. (You may not claim an ownership/lease expense for more than two vehicles.) ☐ 1 ☐ 2 or more. Enter, in Line a below, the "Ownership Costs" for "One Car" from the IRS Local Standards: Transportation (available at www.usdoj.gov/ust/ or from the clerk of the bankruptcy court); enter in Line b the total of the Average Monthly Payments for any debts secured by Vehicle 1, as stated in Line 42; subtract Line b from Line a and enter the result in Line 23. **Do not enter an amount less than zero.**		

a.	IRS Transportation Standards, Ownership Costs	$	
b.	Average Monthly Payment for any debts secured by Vehicle 1, as stated in Line 42	$	
c.	Net ownership/lease expense for Vehicle 1	Subtract Line b from Line a.	$

24	**Local Standards: transportation ownership/lease expense; Vehicle 2.** Complete this Line only if you checked the "2 or more" Box in Line 23. Enter, in Line a below, the "Ownership Costs" for "One Car" from the IRS Local Standards: Transportation (available at www.usdoj.gov/ust/ or from the clerk of the bankruptcy court); enter in Line b the total of the Average Monthly Payments for any debts secured by Vehicle 2, as stated in Line 42; subtract Line b from Line a and enter the result in Line 24. **Do not enter an amount less than zero.**

a.	IRS Transportation Standards, Ownership Costs	$	
b.	Average Monthly Payment for any debts secured by Vehicle 2, as stated in Line 42	$	
c.	Net ownership/lease expense for Vehicle 2	Subtract Line b from Line a.	$

25	**Other Necessary Expenses: taxes.** Enter the total average monthly expense that you actually incur for all federal, state and local taxes, other than real estate and sales taxes, such as income taxes, self-employment taxes, social-security taxes, and Medicare taxes. **Do not include real estate or sales taxes.**	$
26	**Other Necessary Expenses: involuntary deductions for employment.** Enter the total average monthly payroll deductions that are required for your employment, such as retirement contributions, union dues, and uniform costs. **Do not include discretionary amounts, such as voluntary 401(k) contributions.**	$
27	**Other Necessary Expenses: life insurance.** Enter total average monthly premiums that you actually pay for term life insurance for yourself. **Do not include premiums for insurance on your dependents, for whole life or for any other form of insurance.**	$
28	**Other Necessary Expenses: court-ordered payments.** Enter the total monthly amount that you are required to pay pursuant to the order of a court or administrative agency, such as spousal or child support payments. **Do not include payments on past due obligations included in Line 44.**	$
29	**Other Necessary Expenses: education for employment or for a physically or mentally challenged child.** Enter the total average monthly amount that you actually expend for education that is a condition of employment and for education that is required for a physically or mentally challenged dependent child for whom no public education providing similar services is available.	$
30	**Other Necessary Expenses: childcare.** Enter the total average monthly amount that you actually expend on childcare—such as baby-sitting, day care, nursery and preschool. **Do not include other educational payments.**	$
31	**Other Necessary Expenses: health care.** Enter the total average monthly amount that you actually expend on health care that is required for the health and welfare of yourself or your dependents, that is not reimbursed by insurance or paid by a health savings account, and that is in excess of the amount entered in Line 19B. **Do not include payments for health insurance or health savings accounts listed in Line 34.**	$
32	**Other Necessary Expenses: telecommunication services.** Enter the total average monthly amount that you actually pay for telecommunication services other than your basic home telephone and cell phone service—such as pagers, call waiting, caller id, special long distance, or internet service—to the extent necessary for your health and welfare or that of your dependents. **Do not include any amount previously deducted.**	$
33	**Total Expenses Allowed under IRS Standards.** Enter the total of Lines 19 through 32.	$

B22A (Official Form 22A) (Chapter 7) (12/08) 6

	Subpart B: Additional Living Expense Deductions **Note: Do not include any expenses that you have listed in Lines 19-32**	
34	**Health Insurance, Disability Insurance, and Health Savings Account Expenses.** List the monthly expenses in the categories set out in lines a-c below that are reasonably necessary for yourself, your spouse, or your dependents. | a.	Health Insurance	$
b.	Disability Insurance	$
c.	Health Savings Account	$ | Total and enter on Line 34 **If you do not actually expend this total amount,** state your actual total average monthly expenditures in the space below: $ _____	$
35	**Continued contributions to the care of household or family members.** Enter the total average actual monthly expenses that you will continue to pay for the reasonable and necessary care and support of an elderly, chronically ill, or disabled member of your household or member of your immediate family who is unable to pay for such expenses.	$
36	**Protection against family violence.** Enter the total average reasonably necessary monthly expenses that you actually incurred to maintain the safety of your family under the Family Violence Prevention and Services Act or other applicable federal law. The nature of these expenses is required to be kept confidential by the court.	$
37	**Home energy costs.** Enter the total average monthly amount, in excess of the allowance specified by IRS Local Standards for Housing and Utilities, that you actually expend for home energy costs. **You must provide your case trustee with documentation of your actual expenses, and you must demonstrate that the additional amount claimed is reasonable and necessary.**	$
38	**Education expenses for dependent children less than 18.** Enter the total average monthly expenses that you actually incur, not to exceed $137.50 per child, for attendance at a private or public elementary or secondary school by your dependent children less than 18 years of age. **You must provide your case trustee with documentation of your actual expenses, and you must explain why the amount claimed is reasonable and necessary and not already accounted for in the IRS Standards.**	$
39	**Additional food and clothing expense.** Enter the total average monthly amount by which your food and clothing expenses exceed the combined allowances for food and clothing (apparel and services) in the IRS National Standards, not to exceed 5% of those combined allowances. (This information is available at www.usdoj.gov/ust/ or from the clerk of the bankruptcy court.) **You must demonstrate that the additional amount claimed is reasonable and necessary.**	$
40	**Continued charitable contributions.** Enter the amount that you will continue to contribute in the form of cash or financial instruments to a charitable organization as defined in 26 U.S.C. § 170(c)(1)-(2).	$
41	**Total Additional Expense Deductions under § 707(b).** Enter the total of Lines 34 through 40	$

	Subpart C: Deductions for Debt Payment				
42	**Future payments on secured claims.** For each of your debts that is secured by an interest in property that you own, list the name of the creditor, identify the property securing the debt, state the Average Monthly Payment, and check whether the payment includes taxes or insurance. The Average Monthly Payment is the total of all amounts scheduled as contractually due to each Secured Creditor in the 60 months following the filing of the bankruptcy case, divided by 60. If necessary, list additional entries on a separate page. Enter the total of the Average Monthly Payments on Line 42.				

		Name of Creditor	Property Securing the Debt	Average Monthly Payment	Does payment include taxes or insurance?
	a.			$	☐ yes ☐ no
	b.			$	☐ yes ☐ no
	c.			$	☐ yes ☐ no
				Total: Add Lines a, b and c.	$

	Other payments on secured claims. If any of debts listed in Line 42 are secured by your primary residence, a motor vehicle, or other property necessary for your support or the support of your dependents, you may include in your deduction 1/60th of any amount (the "cure amount") that you must pay the creditor in addition to the payments listed in Line 42, in order to maintain possession of the property. The cure amount would include any sums in default that must be paid in order to avoid repossession or foreclosure. List and total any such amounts in the following chart. If necessary, list additional entries on a separate page.		

		Name of Creditor	Property Securing the Debt	1/60th of the Cure Amount
43	a.			$
	b.			$
	c.			$
			Total: Add Lines a, b and c	$

44	**Payments on prepetition priority claims.** Enter the total amount, divided by 60, of all priority claims, such as priority tax, child support and alimony claims, for which you were liable at the time of your bankruptcy filing. **Do not include current obligations, such as those set out in Line 28.**	$

45	**Chapter 13 administrative expenses.** If you are eligible to file a case under chapter 13, complete the following chart, multiply the amount in line a by the amount in line b, and enter the resulting administrative expense.	

	a.	Projected average monthly chapter 13 plan payment.	$
	b.	Current multiplier for your district as determined under schedules issued by the Executive Office for United States Trustees. (This information is available at www.usdoj.gov/ust/ or from the clerk of the bankruptcy court.)	x
	c.	Average monthly administrative expense of chapter 13 case	Total: Multiply Lines a and b

46	**Total Deductions for Debt Payment.** Enter the total of Lines 42 through 45.	$

	Subpart D: Total Deductions from Income	
47	**Total of all deductions allowed under § 707(b)(2).** Enter the total of Lines 33, 41, and 46.	$

B22A (Official Form 22A) (Chapter 7) (12/08)   8

	Part VI. DETERMINATION OF § 707(b)(2) PRESUMPTION	
48	Enter the amount from Line 18 (Current monthly income for § 707(b)(2))	$
49	Enter the amount from Line 47 (Total of all deductions allowed under § 707(b)(2))	$
50	Monthly disposable income under § 707(b)(2). Subtract Line 49 from Line 48 and enter the result	$
51	**60-month disposable income under § 707(b)(2).** Multiply the amount in Line 50 by the number 60 and enter the result.	$
52	**Initial presumption determination.** Check the applicable box and proceed as directed. ☐ **The amount on Line 51 is less than $6,575** Check the box for "The presumption does not arise" at the top of page 1 of this statement, and complete the verification in Part VIII. Do not complete the remainder of Part VI. ☐ **The amount set forth on Line 51 is more than $10,950.** Check the box for "The presumption arises" at the top of page 1 of this statement, and complete the verification in Part VIII. You may also complete Part VII. Do not complete the remainder of Part VI. ☐ **The amount on Line 51 is at least $6,575, but not more than $10,950.** Complete the remainder of Part VI (Lines 53 through 55).	
53	Enter the amount of your total non-priority unsecured debt	$
54	**Threshold debt payment amount.** Multiply the amount in Line 53 by the number 0.25 and enter the result.	$
55	**Secondary presumption determination.** Check the applicable box and proceed as directed. ☐ **The amount on Line 51 is less than the amount on Line 54.** Check the box for "The presumption does not arise" at the top of page 1 of this statement, and complete the verification in Part VIII. ☐ **The amount on Line 51 is equal to or greater than the amount on Line 54.** Check the box for "The presumption arises" at the top of page 1 of this statement, and complete the verification in Part VIII. You may also complete Part VII.	

	Part VII: ADDITIONAL EXPENSE CLAIMS		
56	**Other Expenses.** List and describe any monthly expenses, not otherwise stated in this form, that are required for the health and welfare of you and your family and that you contend should be an additional deduction from your current monthly income under § 707(b)(2)(A)(ii)(I). If necessary, list additional sources on a separate page. All figures should reflect your average monthly expense for each item. Total the expenses.		

		Expense Description	Monthly Amount
	a.		$
	b.		$
	c.		$
		Total: Add Lines a, b and c	$

	Part VIII: VERIFICATION

57	I declare under penalty of perjury that the information provided in this statement is true and correct. *(If this is a joint case, both debtors must sign.)*
	
	Date: _____ Signature: _____
	                                        (Debtor)
	
	Date: _____ Signature: _____
	                                        (Joint Debtor, if any)

Appendix B

Bankruptcy Information Sheet

BANKRUPTCY LAW IS A FEDERAL LAW. THIS SHEET GIVES YOU SOME GENERAL INFORMATION ABOUT WHAT HAPPENS IN A BANKRUPTCY CASE. THE INFORMATION HERE IS NOT COMPLETE. YOU MAY NEED LEGAL ADVICE.

When You File Bankruptcy

You can choose the kind of bankruptcy that best meets your needs (provided you meet certain qualifications):

Chapter 7 – A trustee is appointed to take over your property. Any property of value will be sold or turned into money to pay your creditors. You may be able to keep some personal items and possibly real estate, depending on the law of the State where you live and applicable federal laws.

Chapter 13 – You can usually keep your property, but you must earn wages or have some other source of regular income and must agree to pay part of your income to your creditors. The court must approve your repayment plan and your budget. A trustee is appointed and will collect the payments from you, pay your creditors, and make sure you live up to the terms of your repayment plan.

Chapter 12 – Like chapter 13, but is only for family farmers and family fishermen.

Chapter 11 – This is used mostly by businesses. In Chapter 11, you may continue to operate your business, but your creditors and the court must approve a plan to repay your debts. There is no trustee unless the judge decides that one is necessary; if a trustee is appointed, the trustee takes control of your business and property.

If you've already filed bankruptcy under chapter 7, you may be able to change your case to another chapter.

Your bankruptcy may be reported on your credit record for as long as ten years. It can affect your ability to receive credit in the future.

What Is a Bankruptcy Discharge and How Does It Operate?

One of the reasons people file bankruptcy is to get a "discharge." A discharge is a court order which states you do not have to pay most of your debts. Some debts cannot be discharged. For example, you cannot discharge debts for–

- most taxes;
- child support;
- alimony;
- most student loans;
- court fines and criminal restitution; and
- personal injury caused by driving drunk or under the influence of drugs.

The discharge only applies to debts that arose before the date you filed. Also, if the judge finds you received money or property by fraud, that debt may not be discharged.

It is important to list all your property and debts in your Bankruptcy schedules. If you do not list a debt, for example, it is possible the debt will not be discharged. The judge can also deny your discharge if you do something dishonest in connection with your Bankruptcy case, such as destroy or hide property, falsify records, lie, or disobey a court order.

You can only receive a Chapter 7 discharge once every eight years. Other rules may apply if you previously received a discharge in a Chapter 13 case. No one can make you pay a debt that has been discharged, but you can voluntarily pay any debt you wish to pay. You do not have to sign a Reaffirmation Agreement (see below) or any other kind of document to do this.

Some creditors hold a secured claim (for example, the bank that holds the mortgage on your house or the loan company that has a lien on your car). You do not have to pay a secured claim if the debt is discharged, but the creditor can still take the property.

What Is a Reaffirmation Agreement?

Even if a debt can be discharged, you may have special reasons why you want to promise to pay it. For example, you may want to work out a plan with the bank to keep your car. To promise to pay that debt, you must sign and file a Reaffirmation Agreement with the court. Reaffirmation

Agreements are under special rules and are voluntary. They are not required by Bankruptcy law or by any other law. Reaffirmation Agreements–

- must be voluntary;
- must not place too heavy a burden on you or your family;
- must be in your best interest; and
- can be canceled anytime before the court issues your discharge or within 60 days after the agreement is filed with the court, whichever gives you the most time.

If you are an individual and not represented by an attorney, the court must hold a hearing to decide whether to approve the Reaffirmation Agreement. The agreement will not be legally binding until the court approves it.

If you reaffirm a debt and then fail to pay it, you owe the debt the same as though there was no Bankruptcy. The debt will not be discharged and the creditor can take action to recover any property on which it has a lien or mortgage. The creditor can also take legal action to recover a judgment against you.

IF YOU WANT MORE INFORMATION OR HAVE ANY QUESTIONS ABOUT HOW THE BANKRUPTCY LAWS AFFECT YOU, YOU MAY NEED LEGAL ADVICE. THE TRUSTEE IN YOUR CASE IS NOT RESPONSIBLE FOR GIVING YOU LEGAL ADVICE.

IMPORTANT INFORMATION ABOUT
BANKRUPTCY ASSISTANCE SERVICES
FROM AN ATTORNEY OR BANKRUPTCY PETITION PREPARER:

If you decide to seek bankruptcy relief, you can represent yourself, you can hire an attorney to represent you, or you can get help in some localities from a Bankruptcy petition preparer who is not an attorney. THE LAW REQUIRES AN ATTORNEY OR BANKRUPTCY PETITION PREPARER TO GIVE YOU A WRITTEN CONTRACT SPECIFYING WHAT THE ATTORNEY OR BANKRUPTCY PETITION PREPARER WILL DO FOR YOU AND HOW MUCH IT WILL COST. Ask to see the contract before you hire anyone.

The following information helps you understand what must be done in a routine Bankruptcy case to help you evaluate how much service you need. Although Bankruptcy can be complex, many cases are routine.

Before filing a Bankruptcy case, either you or your attorney should analyze your eligibility for different forms of debt relief available under the Bankruptcy Code and which form of relief is most likely to be beneficial for you. Be sure you understand the relief you can obtain and its limitations. To file a Bankruptcy case, documents called a Petition, Schedules and Statement of Financial Affairs, as well as in some cases a Statement of Intention need to be prepared correctly and filed with the Bankruptcy Court. You will have to pay a filing fee to the Bankruptcy Court. Once your case starts, you will have to attend the required first meeting of creditors where you may be questioned by a court official called a "trustee" and by creditors.

If you choose to file a chapter 7 case, you may be asked by a creditor to reaffirm a debt. You may want help deciding whether to do so. A creditor is not permitted to coerce you into reaffirming your debts.

If you choose to file a Chapter 13 case in which you repay your creditors what you can afford over three to five years, you may also want help with preparing your Chapter 13 plan and with the confirmation hearing on your planM which will be before a bankruptcy judge.

If you select another type of relief under the Bankruptcy Code other than Chapter 7 or Chapter 13, you will want to find out what should be done from someone familiar with that type of relief.

Your Bankruptcy case may also involve litigation. You are generally permitted to represent yourself in litigation in Bankruptcy court, but only attorneys, not Bankruptcy petition preparers, can give you legal advice.

Appendix C:

The Federal Bankruptcy Exemptions

Code Citation	kind of property	maximum value per person
11 USC sec. 522(d)(1)	your home, including a coop or a manufactured home; a burial plot	$20,200.00
11 USC sec. 522(d)(2)	one motor vehicle per person	$3,225.00
11 USC sec. 522(d)(3)	household goods, furnishings, clothing, appliances, books, animals, crops or musical instruments where no one piece of property is worth more than $525	$10,775.00
11 USC sec. 522(d)(4)	jewelry	$1,350.00
11 USC sec. 522(d)(5)	wildcard - anything	$1075 plus unused portion of exemption (1) up to $10,125
11 USC sec. 522(d)(6)	"tools of the trade" - tools and books you use for work	$2,025.00
11 USC sec. 522(d)(7)	life insurance - not including "cash value" or "whole life" policies	no limit
11 USC sec. 522(d)(8)	cash value life insurance policy	$10,775.00
11 USC sec. 522(d)(9)	health aids professionally prescribed for you or a dependent	no limit
11 USC sec. 522(d)(10)	Social Security, veterans' benefit, disability/illness/unemployment benefit, alimony/child support, pension plan	no limit
11 USC sec. 522(d)(11)	Certain lawsuit awards - consult your attorney on this one	
11 USC sec. 522(d)(12)	401Ks, 401As, IRAs, pension funds, retirement savings	no limit

Appendix D:

Sample Declaration of Separate Households

UNITED STATES BANKRUPTCY COURT
EASTERN DISTRICT OF MICHIGAN
SOUTHERN DIVISION

In re:	)	
Joseph Allan Sample, Jr.	)	Chapter 7
(DBA The Sample Company)	)	
Debtor	)	

AFFIDAVIT OF SEPARATE HOUSEHOLDS

I, Joseph Allan Sample, Jr., being duly sworn, depose and state as follows

1.   That I am the Debtor above.

2.   That my wife and I are separated.

3.   That as a result, my wife and I keep our finances separate.

4.   That as a result, we maintain separate households.

Further, affiant sayeth naught.

_____

Joseph Allan Sample, Jr.

Signed and sworn before me on May 2, 2010.

_____

Signed, Notary Public

About the Author

Michael Greiner is a bankruptcy attorney and the founder and president of the Financial Law Group, P.C. Since the change in bankruptcy law a few years ago, Mike has represented over 1000 individuals, businesses, and creditors in bankruptcy court. He created the website myeasy7.com to help people file Chapter 7 Bankruptcy on their own. Before starting his practice, Greiner spent more than fifteen years in politics and government. He is married to Madilyn, with whom he has two children, Kelsey and Jack.

INDEX

Available from NorlightsPress and fine booksellers everywhere

Toll free: 888-558-4354   **Online:** www.norlightspress.com

Shipping Info:
   Add $2.95 for first item and $1.00 for each additional item

Name _____

Address _____

Daytime Phone _____

E-mail _____

No. Copies	Title	Price (each)	Total Cost

	Subtotal	
	Shipping	
	Total	

Payment by (circle one):
   Check   Visa   Mastercard   Discover   Am Express

Card number_____3 digit code_____

Exp.date_____ Signature_____

Mailing Address:

2721 Tulip Tree Rd.
Nashville, IN 47448

Sign up to receive our catalogue at www.norlightspress.com

LaVergne, TN USA
20 November 2010

205714LV00005B/200/P